CAST IRON DUTCH OVEN CAMPING
COOKBOOK

NOURISHING MEALS FROM CAST IRON DUTCH OVEN COOKING UNDER THE OPEN SKY

EVERLEE SANDERS

Copyright

TABLE OF CONTENTS

INTRODUCTION

Welcome to the Cast Iron Dutch Oven Camping Cookbook, where the smell of cooking outside meets the sound of a campfire in the middle of the night. This cookbook, which outdoor enthusiast Everlee Sanders wrote, is a celebration of healthy meals made with the classic charm of cooking in a cast iron dutch oven.

In this book, you'll go on a culinary adventure through the wilderness, learning how much fun it is to make healthy meals in the great outdoors. Whether you've been camping for years or this is your first time, the recipes in these pages are meant to inspire and delight, taking your camping experience to a whole new level.

Each recipe, from hearty breakfasts to filling dinners and sweet treats, has been carefully crafted to be cooked over an open flame or nestled into the coals of a campfire. This way, the rich flavors of cooking outside are added to every dish.

Start with Appetizers & Snacks, then move on to Soups & Stews, Veggies & Side Dishes, Main Dishes, Fish & Seafood, Beef & Pork, and Poultry & Lamb. And finally, Desserts. For every craving and every adventure, this cookbook has something for you. Start your day with a hot skillet breakfast, enjoy a hearty stew as the sun goes down, or treat yourself to a rich dessert under the stars.

So, get together around the campfire with your cast iron Dutch oven, get ready to make memories, and eat healthy meals in the great outdoors. The Cast Iron Dutch Oven Camping Cookbook will help you find culinary bliss in the great outdoors.

WHAT IS CAST IRON DUTCH OVEN?

A Dutch oven made of cast iron is a versatile cooking pot that has been used for hundreds of years in many cultures around the world. It's usually made up of a pot with thick walls and a lid that fits tightly on top. The cast iron that was used to make it keeps and spreads heat very well, making it perfect for cooking many different foods.

The term "Dutch oven" comes from the 17th century, when Dutch metalworkers were known for how well they could cast metal. For cooking, these early Dutch ovens were often made with legs that let them sit directly on coals or in a fireplace.

These days, cast iron There are many shapes and sizes of Dutch ovens, but they all have the same basic features. They're strong, can handle high temperatures, and can be used on stoves, in ovens, and even over open flames. This makes them a popular choice for cooking while camping or outside.

Stainless steel Dutch ovens are admired for their ability to spread heat evenly, which makes cooking slowly and evenly bring out the flavors of the food. Many people use them for cooking meats, cooking bread, simmering soups and stews, and even frying food.

Cast iron Dutch ovens are very popular in the kitchen because they are durable, can be used for many tasks, and make hearty, tasty meals.

BENEFITS OF CAST IRON DUTCH OVEN?

Iron ore Dutch ovens are popular among cooks because they have a number of advantages:

Excellent at Holding Heat: Cast iron is famous for keeping heat in and making cooking even and consistent. Because of this, Dutch ovens are great for cooking things like stews, soups, and braises that need to be cooked slowly over a long period of time.

Versatility: Dutch ovens can be used on stoves, in ovens, or over campfires, among other heat sources. Because of this, they can be used for many types of cooking, from baking and frying to simmering and braising. Cast iron is durable. If you take good care of your Dutch oven, it can last for generations. Because they don't scratch, dent, or warp easily, they will last for a long time in your kitchen.

Natural Nonstick Properties: Once cast iron has been properly seasoned, it develops a naturally nonstick surface. This means that you can use less oil or butter when cooking. This makes it a great choice for cooking because food won't stick to the surface when you fry or sauté it.

Adds Iron to Food: Cooking with cast iron can make your food contain more iron, which is good for people who are at risk of not getting enough iron. This is usually true when cooking acidic foods like tomatoes, which can help the iron leave the pan.

Improves Flavor: Food cooked in cast iron has a unique flavor that is often described as rich and earthy. This gives food more depth and complexity, which makes it taste better and more enjoyable.

Easy to Clean: Cast iron needs some upkeep to stay in good shape, but it's pretty easy to clean. Just use hot water to rinse and a soft brush or sponge to scrub. Do not use soap because it can take away the seasoning.

The benefits of cast iron Dutch ovens make them a useful and important kitchen tool that can make cooking delicious meals easy.

HOW TO CLEAN CAST IRON DUTCH OVEN?

A cast iron Dutch oven is easy to clean, but there are a few important steps you should take to keep it from rusting and to keep the seasoning. Here's how to clean your Dutch oven made of cast iron:

Cool Down: After cooking, let the Dutch oven cool down all the way. If you try to clean it while it's still hot, you could get burned or damage it.
If any food residue is left on the Dutch oven's surface, use a wooden or silicone spatula to scrape it off. Do not use metal tools because they can ruin the seasoning.

Rinse with Hot Water: Running hot water over the Dutch oven will get rid of any loose food. Do not use soap because it can take away the seasoning. You can gently scrub the surface with a soft brush or sponge if you need to.

Dry Fully: Use a clean towel to dry the Dutch oven. To keep the pot from rusting, make sure that all the water is gone from the inside and the outside.
If you think the seasoning on your Dutch oven isn't as good as it could be, or if you see any signs of rust, you may need to re-season it. To do this, cover the whole Dutch oven, including the lid, with a thin layer of vegetable oil or melted shortening. Turn it over and put it in an oven that is already hot (375°F/190°C) for about an hour. Let it cool all the way down before putting it away.

How to Store It: Keep your cast iron Dutch oven somewhere dry and open the lid so air can flow through it. Do not put other pots or pans on top of it; this could damage the seasoning.

These steps will help you clean your cast iron Dutch oven properly so that it stays strong and doesn't stick for years to come. Remember that taking good care of and maintaining your cast iron cookware is very important if you want to keep its quality.

1. MOUNTAIN MAN BREAKFAST CASSEROLE

Prep Time: 10 Minutes | Cook Time: 25 Minutes

Total Time: 35 Minutes | Serving: 8

Ingredients

- 1 large onion, chopped
- salt and pepper to taste
- 1 Dozen eggs, whisked
- 1 pound pork sausage
- 1 cup of diced cheddar cheese
- 2 packages Simply Potatoes, hash browns or diced

Instructions

1. Over a hot coal fire, brown the sausage in a cast iron Dutch oven. Take the sausage out and let it drain on paper towels.
2. In the remaining fat, cook the onion until it's soft. Stir in the potatoes until they are crispy and just a little brown. Cover the bottom with potatoes and add the sausage, eggs, and cheese on top. Add 16 hot coals to the lid and then put it on top.
3. Put the eggs in the oven and bake for 25 minutes until they are set. Help yourself!

2. MONKEY BREAD

Prep Time: 5 Minutes | Cook Time: 15 Minutes

Total Time: 20 Minutes | Serving: 6

Ingredients

- ➢ 1/2 cup of chopped walnuts
- ➢ 2 tbsp cinnamon
- ➢ 1/4 cup of brown sugar
- ➢ 4 tbsp butter (that is 1/2 stick butter)
- ➢ 1 (16 ounce) tube refrigerator biscuits
- ➢ 1/4 cup of white sugar
- ➢ Powdered sugar glaze

Instructions

1. On a total of 25 coals (17 on the top of the lid and 8 below the bottom of the oven), heat the Dutch oven up to 350 degrees F.
2. In a plastic bag, mix vanilla sugar, brown sugar, cinnamon, and nuts.
3. To make a good coating, tear each biscuit into small pieces and drop them into the bag. Make sure the bag is tight so you don't make a mess, and then shake it to mix the pieces well.
4. The butter should be melted in the Dutch oven.
5. Pour the whole bag into the oven, stir it with butter, and then spread it out on the bottom to make a single, even layer.
6. There will be 15 to 25 minutes of cooking time at 350 degrees F with the lid on. Placement of the coals: Make sure the bottom coals are set up in a circle so there is no "center coal." If there is a center coal, the bread pieces in the middle will catch fire.
7. Alternately turn the oven's lid and bottom every five minutes to make sure the baking is even.
8. Take it off the heat and let it cool a bit before serving it hot.
9. If you want, you can put a powdered sugar glaze on top.

3. COFFEE CAKE

Prep Time: 15 Minutes | Cook Time: 20 Minutes

Total Time: 35 Minutes | Serving: 6

Ingredients

- 1 cup of chopped pecans
- 4 eggs beaten
- 1 tbsp ground cinnamon
- 3/4 cup of vegetable oil
- 1 box yellow cake mix
- 1 tsp vanilla
- 1 (8 ounce) container sour cream
- 1 cup of brown sugar

For serving:

- 3 tbsp powdered sugar
- For baking without a parchment paper liner:
- Vegetable spray (use non-stick spray if baking directly in your Dutch oven, or, line it with a parchment paper liner)

Instructions

1. Stir the cake mix, pecans, vegetable oil, eggs, sour cream, and vanilla together in a medium-sized bowl. Set this bowl aside.
2. If you're using parchment paper, put it in the oven. Warm up a 10-inch camp Dutch oven to 325 degrees. This will take 19 charcoal briquettes, 13 on top of the lid and 6 below the bottom of the oven.
3. Vegetable spray should be used to line your Dutch oven if you are not using parchment paper.
4. Put the batter in the oven's bottom.
5. Put the batter in the oven and sprinkle the brown sugar on top of it.
6. Put the lid on top and bake at 325 degrees for 20-30 minutes, or until it's done. The exact time will depend on your altitude and the temperature of the air outside.
7. During the cooking process, turn the oven and lid 1/4 turn in opposite directions. This simple coffee cake is done when you stick a knife in the center of it and it comes out clean.
8. Take the Dutch oven off the coals and take off the lid to let it cool down a bit. Take the cake out of the oven to cool if you used a parchment paper liner.
9. Mix powdered sugar into the cake, then cut it up and serve.

4. SPRING GREEN CAMPFIRE FRITTATA

Prep Time: 15 Minutes | Cook Time: 30 Minutes

Total Time: 45 Minutes | Serving: 4

Ingredients

- ➢ 1 cup of grated cheddar cheese
- ➢ 1 cup of sliced mushrooms – any kind
- ➢ Tabasco for serving
- ➢ 1 avocado for serving
- ➢ 1/4 tsp freshly ground black pepper
- ➢ 6 small green onions ends trimmed
- ➢ fresh mild herbs such as parsley or basil
- ➢ 1/4 tsp fine sea salt
- ➢ 10 large eggs
- ➢ 8 slices bacon
- ➢ chive blossoms optional
- ➢ 1 small bundle asparagus ends snapped off
- ➢ 1 handful fresh cherry tomatoes

Instructions

1. Use a camp stove or fire to heat a cast iron Dutch oven. Over medium-high temperature, add the bacon and cook until almost crispy. Take it out of the pot and set it aside. Pour some of the fat into a small jar and set the rest aside. Leave a little fat in the pot.
2. Add the asparagus and green onion to the pot. When you cook them together, turn them over every so often until the asparagus turns bright green and the green onion wilts. Add the mushrooms and cook for one or two minutes. Take everything out of the pot and wrap it in tin foil to keep it heated.
3. With a fork, break the eggs into a bowl just enough to separate the yolks. Tear the herbs up and add them to the eggs. Add salt and pepper to taste.
4. Spread out a tsp of bacon fat on the bottom and sides of the pot by swirling it around. Second, add half of the egg. Next, arrange the mushrooms, asparagus, and green onions on top of the egg. Do not include any juices that may have collected under the vegetables. Cover the vegetables with three-quarters of the cheese. Pour the rest of the beaten egg on top. Put the bacon back in the pot. Add the cherry tomatoes and the rest of the cheese on top. If you have any herbs left over, add them.
5. Place the pot over low heat (low coals, not full flame) with the lid on. To carefully put embers on the lid, use a strong pair of tongs. Cover and cook for 30 minutes or until the egg is almost done. Check under the lid often to see how the eggs are cooking because the time will depend on how hot the campfire. Take it off the heat and cover it for about 10 minutes. During this time of rest, the eggs will keep cooking.
6. Cut the frittata into four equal parts and serve hot with Tabasco and avocado slices. If you need, you can add fresh herbs or chive blossoms at the end.

5. FRENCH TOAST BAKE

Prep Time: 5 Minutes | Cook Time: 30 Minutes

Total Time: 35 Minutes | Serving: 4

Ingredients

- 1 cup of milk
- ¾ cup of blueberries
- 8 slices thick bread
- ¼ tsp salt
- 1 tbsp vanilla extract
- ¼ cup of sugar
- 3 eggs
- 2 tbsp cinnamon

Instructions

1. Light your coals. Cut out a circle of parchment paper to line the inside of a 10-inch Dutch oven.
2. Cut the bread into rough squares about 2 inches across and put them on top of the parchment paper in the Dutch oven.
3. Add the eggs to a large bowl and mix them well. Then add the salt, sugar, cinnamon, and vanilla extract and mix them in. Once all of those things are mixed in, add the milk and stir.
4. Now, add the mixture to the bread slowly. A wooden spoon or rubber spatula can be used to gently toss the bread so that all of the pieces are covered. Put the blueberries on top and mix it in slowly.
5. Place the Dutch oven on top of seven evenly spaced briquettes and cover it. Then, add 14 briquettes to the top of the lid to make an oven that is about 10 inches deep and 350 degrees. For an 8-inch oven, use 16 coals, and for a 12-inch oven, use 25 coals. Put about a third of the coals on top and the rest on the bottom. Put it in the oven for 30 minutes. Add maple syrup and butter to taste.

6. OLD FASHIONED APPLE FRITTERS

Prep Time: 15 Minutes | Cook Time: 20 Minutes

Total Time: 35 Minutes | Serving: 3 Fritters

Ingredients

- 1 tsp cinnamon
- 3 tbsp light brown sugar
- 3 cups of apples, diced
- 2 Eggs
- 1 tsp vanilla extract
- 1 cup of all-purpose flour
- 1/4 tsp salt
- 2 tsp baking powder
- vegetable oil for frying
- 1/4 cup of milk

For the Glaze:

- 3-4 tsp water
- 1 tsp vanilla extract
- 1 1/2 cup of powdered sugar

Instructions

1. Mix the baking powder, flour, salt, and cinnamon in a large bowl. Mix them together using a whisk.
2. In a medium-sized bowl, mix the sugar, eggs, and vanilla together using an electric whisk.
3. Mix the flour and eggs together and stir until the mixture is smooth. Then add the milk and mix it in.
4. Just cover the inapples with the folds. Assemble the ingredients well.
5. There should be at least 2 inches of vegetable-based oil in a Dutch oven or cast iron pot. Heat it on medium-high until it reaches 350°F.
6. Dollop the batter into the oil with a cookie scoop or a tbsp. Cook three to four at a time. The fritters should be cooked for about 4-5 minutes, turning them over every two minutes, until they are a deep golden brown color.
7. In a tray lined with paper towels, take the fritters out of the oil using the spider tool.
8. Mix powdered sugar, water, and vanilla extract together to make the glaze. In the glaze, dip the fritters. Happy eating!

7. BABY PANCAKE

Prep Time: 5 Minutes | Cook Time: 20 Minutes

Total Time: 25 Minutes | Serving: 4

Ingredients

- 3 tbsp sugar
- 3 tbsp unsalted butter
- Pinch of salt
- ½ cup of all-purpose flour
- ½ tsp vanilla extract
- 2 large eggs at room temperature
- ½ cup of whole milk at room temperature

Toppings (Pick your favorite):

- Jam
- 3 cups of mixed berries or other fruit
- Confectioners' sugar
- Lemon wedges

Instructions

1. Warm the oven up to 375 degrees Fahrenheit.
2. To make the batter smooth, put the eggs, flour, sugar, salt, milk, and vanilla in a blender and blend them all together. You can also do this by hand.
3. Doing this on the stove or in a 10-inch cast iron skillet or baking dish is possible. Put the butter in the pan and bake it. The skillet will be too hot, so be careful when you take it out of the oven after the butter has melted. Then, add the pancake batter. Put the pan back in the oven and bake for 20 minutes or until the edges are golden and the center is puffed up. Don't open the oven door while it's baking. Take it out of the oven and serve it with berries, lemon wedges, and confectioners' sugar on top.

8. CINNAMON ROLLS

Prep Time: 30 Minutes | Cook Time: 45 Minutes

Total Time: 1 Hour 15 Minutes | Serving: 1

Ingredients

Dough:

- ➤ 1 tsp cinnamon
- ➤ ¾ cup of milk, preferably whole
- ➤ 3 tbsp granulated sugar, (50g)
- ➤ ½ tsp sea salt
- ➤ 2 tsp active dry yeast, or 1 packet
- ➤ 2 ½ cups of flour, (345g)
- ➤ 1 egg
- ➤ 4 tbsp butter

Filling:

- ➤ 4 cardamom pods
- ➤ ⅓ cup of brown sugar (packed), (70g)
- ➤ 1 tbsp ground cinnamon
- ➤ 4 Tbsp butter, softened

Icing Glaze:

- ➤ 1 tbsp milk
- ➤ ½ cup of powdered sugar
- ➤ 1 tbsp melted butter

Instructions

1. Take the rolls out of the cooler and put them in a Dutch oven that holds 4 quarts. Add the lid on the oven and let the dough rise while you start the fire or coals.
2. When the coals are hot, put seven of them in a circle around the Dutch oven. Add 16 more on top of the lid. Place in the oven and bake for 30 to 45 minutes, or until the tops turn golden. Take it off the heat.
3. Do this step if you don't already have it done at home, and then drizzle the icing over the rolls. Have a hot cup of camp coffee!

9. FRENCH TOAST CASSEROLE

Prep Time: 5 Minutes | Cook Time: 1 Hour | Additional Time: 4 Hour

Total Time: 5 Hour 5 Minutes | Serving: 6

Ingredients

- 1 cup of brown sugar
- 1 tsp vanilla
- 1/2 cup of butter, melted
- 1 tsp cinnamon
- 1 loaf French baguette, in 1" slices
- 6 eggs
- 1/2 cup of pecans
- 1 cup of milk
- 1 cup of syrup

Instructions

1. Put parchment paper around the edges of a Dutch oven. Do not have to, but this makes it easy to clean up later.
2. In the Dutch oven's bottom, put the butter, sugar, pecans, and half of the syrup.
3. Put the slices of baguette on top of the butter and sugar mixture.
4. Add the eggs, milk, cinnamon, and vanilla to a bowl and whisk them together. Then, pour the mixture over the bread. Put it in the fridge for at least 4 hours or overnight.
5. Tip: When we go camping in the fall and winter, we just leave the Dutch oven outside in the cold, where animals can't get to it.
6. Put it in an oven set to 350 degrees or over a campfire for an hour.
7. Add the rest of the syrup on top, and serve.

10. BREAKFAST BAKE

Prep Time: 10 Minutes | Cook Time: 1 Hour

Total Time: 1 Hour 10 Minutes | Serving: 1

Ingredients

- 8 Eggs
- 1/2 White onion, diced
- 1 Bell pepper, diced
- 2 cups of Tatertot hash browns
- 1/2 cup of Cheese, shredded
- 2 Green onion stalks, diced
- Salt & pepper
- 1/2 cup of Cooked ham, diced

Instructions

1. Cut the ham, pepper, and onion into small pieces. Put the cheese, salt, and pepper to the egg. Put the ingredients in a big freezer bag so they are easy to store and pack.
2. You don't have to line a Dutch oven with parchment paper, but it will make it easier to clean up and serve later. Put tater tots in a layer on the bottom of the Dutch oven.
3. The egg mix should be poured over the hash browns.
4. Put the lid on top of the Dutch oven and bake it for an hour over a campfire or in a 350-degree oven. Before you serve, sprinkle green onions on top.

11. DUTCH BABY

Prep Time: 5 Minutes | Cook Time: 20 Minutes

Total Time: 25 Minutes | Serving: 4

Ingredients

- ¼ tsp salt
- ½ cup of whole milk, at room temperature
- ¼ tsp ground nutmeg, optional
- 3 large eggs, at room temperature
- 1 tbsp sugar
- 4 tbsp unsalted butter
- ½ cup of all-purpose flour

Optional toppings:

- Syrup, fresh fruit, preserves, confectioners' (powdered) sugar, or cinnamon sugar

Instructions

1. Get your coals ready: Light charcoals (which is what you should do) or start a campfire to cook. Setting coals on fire will take 20 minutes, and it could take an hour for a campfire to go out.
2. To make the batter, crack the eggs into a large bowl and beat them very well until they are smooth. Add the milk and stir it in quickly to mix it in. Then add the sugar, salt, flour, and nutmeg. Combine and blend until smooth.
3. Once the coals or embers are ready, put your Dutch oven over temperature to warm it up. Spread the butter out in the Dutch oven and stir it around until it melts. Putting the batter into the Dutch oven after the butter is fully melted.
4. Put the lid on top of the Dutch oven. Place on a small bed of coals, and then add more coals to cover the lid.
5. Take a quick peak every 10 minutes to see how things are going. The Dutch baby should be puffed up and have golden brown spots on it. If you need to, cook for a few more minutes. When it's done, take it off the heat.
6. Serve right away with any toppings you like.

12. BUTTERMILK BISCUITS

Prep Time: 20 Minutes | Cook Time: 15 Minutes

Total Time: 35 Minutes | Serving: 12-16

Ingredients

- 1 tsp salt
- ¾ cup of buttermilk
- ½ cup of butter
- 1 beaten egg
- ¼ cup of melted butter (for top of biscuits)
- ¼ cup of club soda
- 5 cups of Bisquick biscuit mix
- 2.5 tbsp granulated sugar

Instructions

1. Put 8 coals on the bottom of the Lodge Dutch Oven and 17 coals on top of it. Grease and heat it.
2. Mix everything together. Hand-knead the dough until it's smooth. Cover waxed paper with dough and press it down until it's ¾ inch thick. Cookies can be made with a biscuit cutter.
3. Spread the biscuits out on the bottom of the hot Dutch oven. Bake for 12 to 15 minutes, or until they turn golden brown. To avoid burn spots, turn the oven and lid around a lot. Don't forget that they will bake down from the top.
4. Take it off the heat and use ¼ cup of melted butter to cover the golden cookies.

13. CAMPFIRE NACHOS

Prep Time: 5 Minutes | Cook Time: 10 Minutes

Total Time: 15 Minutes | Serving: 2

Ingredients

- ➤ 4-5 green onions, sliced
- ➤ 1 (14.5 ounce) can black beans, drained
- ➤ ½ pound tortilla chips
- ➤ 1 small lime, cut into wedges
- ➤ 1 tbsp neutral flavored oil
- ➤ 1 large avocado, cubed
- ➤ 1 (7.75 ounce) can El Pato hot tomato sauce, or equivalent
- ➤ 1 cup of shredded Mexican cheese blend
- ➤ handful of fresh cilantro, chopped

Instructions

1. To keep the nachos from sticking, lightly oil the bottom of a large Dutch oven.
2. Spread ⅓ of the chips out evenly in the Dutch oven. Add ¼ can of El Pato, ¼ cup of cheese, ¼ can of black beans, and a handful of avocado, green onions, and cilantro on top of the chips. And do it again for the second layer.
3. Add the last ⅓ of the chips, ½ of the black beans, ½ of the El Pato, ½ cup of cheese, and the rest of the avocado, onion, and cilantro for the third and final layer.
4. Cover the Dutch oven and set it on a metal grill over a campfire. Let it sit for 10 minutes or so, until the cheese melts. Put the lime wedges on top.

14. CHEESY PULL APART GARLIC BREAD

Prep Time: 5 Minutes | Cook Time: 15 Minutes

Total Time: 20 Minutes | Serving: 4

Ingredients

- ➤ 6 ounce shredded mozzarella cheese
- ➤ 1 round Italian or sourdough bread loaf
- ➤ 3 large cloves of garlic
- ➤ 1/4 cup of fresh parsley or basil (chopped)
- ➤ 1/4 tsp salt
- ➤ 1/2 cup of unsalted butter

Instructions

1. Remove the butter from the cooler and let it warm up enough to spread.
2. Use a chimney starter to get your briquettes hot. About 22 to 25 briquettes will do.
3. Cut your bread into long, thin slices, but don't go all the way through to the bottom. The loaf should still be able to stay together.
4. Use a lot of the garlic butter you made at home to cover one side of each slice of bread.
5. Lots of shreds of cheese should go on each slice.
6. Finally, cut the bread into bite-sized squares by cutting it vertically but not all the way through to the bottom.
7. Put parchment paper around the edges of your Dutch oven to make it easier to clean, then carefully put your cheese bread inside. Put the lid on top.
8. To get the Dutch oven to 425°F, put briquettes on the top and bottom. Place the dish in the oven and melt the cheese overnight.
9. Take the Dutch oven off the temperature and add chopped basil or parsley to the bread. Enjoy!

15. STEAMED CLAMS

Prep Time: 15 Minutes | Cook Time: 13 Minutes | Total Time: 28 Minutes | Serving: 2

Ingredients

- 2 tbsp butter
- ½ tsp red pepper flakes
- 2 cloves garlic, minced
- ¾ cup of white wine
- 2 pounds littleneck clams
- 1 lemon, cut into quarters
- Crusty baguette, sliced
- fresh parsley

Instructions

1. If any of the clams are open, you can still use them if they close within a few minutes of being tapped. If they don't, you should throw them away. Crack the clams open and wash them.
2. On medium temprature, melt the butter in a Dutch oven or another pan with a lid that fits tightly on top. When the bubbles stop, add the garlic and red pepper flakes and cook for two minutes.
3. After you add the wine, let it boil for about 30 seconds or until the alcohol taste goes away (there should still be liquid in the pot, though!).
4. Insert the clams and cover the pot with a lid. The clams should open after 5 to 10 minutes of steaming. Any clams that are still closed should be thrown away.
5. Include lemon juice, parsley, and grilled bread to soak up all the sauce.

16. JALAPENO POPPERS

Prep Time: 15 Minutes | Cook Time: 35 Minutes | Total Time: 50 Minutes | Serving: 20

Ingredients

- 1 pound bacon regular thickness
- 8 ounce cream cheese softened
- 1 tsp granulated garlic
- 10 Jalapenos sliced in half length wise and seeds removed

Instructions

1. Before you use it, set the cream cheese out to warm up.
2. Warm the oven up to 350°F. Cut the peppers into slices and take out the seeds and veins. Set them aside. In a medium bowl, mix the garlic powder and cream cheese.
3. Add some cream cheese to each Jalapeno slice. Each stuffed Jalapeno should have bacon wrapped around it. Put bacon together with a toothpick.
4. Pop the corn in a 12" camp oven, a 6 quart Dutch oven, or a 12" skillet.
5. The bacon should be cooked all the way through after 35 minutes in the oven.
6. Broil the bacon for one to two minutes to make it extra crispy.
7. Let it sit for a minute or two, then serve and enjoy.

17. ZUCCHINI BREAD

Prep Time: 20 Minutes | Cook Time: 1 Hour

Total Time: 1 Hour 20 Minutes | Serving: 3

Ingredients

- ➢ 2/3 cup of melted butter plus butter to grease pan
- ➢ 1/2 tsp ground cloves
- ➢ 3 cups of whole wheat pastry flour
- ➢ 1 tsp ground cinnamon
- ➢ 1/2 tsp baking powder
- ➢ 2 tsp baking soda
- ➢ 1 tsp sea salt
- ➢ 3 cups of zucchini shredded
- ➢ 1/2 cup of coarsely chopped nuts
- ➢ 2 tsp pure vanilla extract
- ➢ 4 eggs
- ➢ 1 1/2 cup of coconut sugar

Instructions

1. To temperature up a cast iron Dutch oven with legs, put 15 hot coals on the lid and 7 hot coals between the legs under the pot. This will bring the Dutch oven to 350°F. If it gets cold, add a few more briquettes.
2. Melt some butter and put it on the bottom of the Dutch oven.
3. In a large bowl, mix together the eggs, cream cheese, coconut sugar, melted butter, and zucchini.
4. Once everything is well mixed, pour it into a Dutch oven that has already been heated.
5. If you stick a wooden pick in the middle and it comes out clean, it's done baking.
6. Let it cool for 10 minutes. Run a knife along the sides of the bread to make it easier to handle. Flip the Dutch oven over by putting a dish on top of it. The cake is now on the plate. Let it cool down before cutting.

18. PEPPERONI GRILLED CHEESE

Prep Time: 3 Minutes | Cook Time: 5 Minutes

Total Time: 8 Minutes | Serving: 1

Ingredients

Butter Mix:

> ➤ 1 Tsp Parsley Flakes
> ➤ 1 Tsp Garlic minced
> ➤ 1/2 Stick Butter softened

Sandwich:

> ➤ 5 Slices Pepperoni
> ➤ 2 Slices Bread used white
> ➤ 2 Slices Mozzarella
> ➤ Spaghetti Sauce for dipping optional

Instructions

Butter Mix:

1. Put the garlic and parsley to the butter and mix them all together. I like to make this ahead of time and bring it to camp in a dish.

Sandwich:

2. Warm up the pie iron over the fire first.
3. Use your garlic butter mixture to butter one side of two slices of bread.
4. Put one slice of bread in your hot pie iron with the butter side down.
5. On top of the bread in the pie iron, put a slice of mozzarella.
6. Put in four or five pepperoni slices. After that, put another piece of cheese on top.
7. Spread butter on the other piece of bread and place it on top of the cheese. The butter side should be facing out so that it can touch the pie iron.
8. Lock the pie iron shut and hold it over the campfire for five minutes. You should flip it a few times to make sure both sides cook the same.
9. Open it slowly and check to see if the gold is right for you. If not, shut the lid and cook for a little longer.
10. Put some sauce on the side so you can dip your food. This is what I do with spaghetti sauce.

19. GARLIC GRILLED CHEESE PIE IRON

Prep Time: 3 Minutes | Cook Time: 5 Minutes

Total Time: 8 Minutes | Serving: 1

Ingredients

Garlic Butter:

- ➤ 1 Tsp Parsley Flakes
- ➤ 1/2 Stick Butter softened
- ➤ 1 Tsp Garlic minced

Grilled Cheese:

- ➤ 2 Slices Munster Cheese
- ➤ 2 Slices Sandwich Bread

Instructions

Garlic Butter:

1. Once everything for the butter is fully mixed, it's ready to use. Keep in the cooler in a container that won't let air in. The butter mix can be used to make four sandwiches.

Grilled Cheese:

1. Start a fire and give it time to get hot.
2. Use the garlic butter mixture to butter two slices of sandwich bread.
3. In the pie iron, put one slice of butter down.
4. On top of the bread in the pie iron, put both slices of cheese.
5. On top of the cheese, put the other piece of butter bread. Place the butter side of the pie iron to touch the other half of the iron.
6. Hold the iron over the campfire and hot coals with the lid closed. Put it in the oven for five minutes. Make sure to turn it over a few times so that it cooks evenly and doesn't burn.
7. Slowly open the pie iron to check if the crust is golden enough. It's done if it is.

20. GRILLED PIZZA

Prep Time: 30 Minutes | Cook Time: 25 Minutes

Total Time: 55 Minutes | Serving: 1

Ingredients

Dough:

- 1 tbsp Olive Oil
- 1 tsp sugar
- 1 tsp course salt
- 2 Cups warm water
- 4 Cups Flour (King Arthur All Purpose or Bread Flour) divided
- 1 tbsp active dry yeast

Filling:

- 1 tsp paprika
- 24 oz ground lamb
- 3 cloves garlic
- 1 tsp cumin
- ½ tsp pepper
- ½ tsp salt
- 1 large bell pepper
- 2 yellow onions

Instructions

1. Get the dough ready.
2. In a heavy bowl, mix water, yeast, and sugar well. Then, let it sit until the yeast starts to bubble. Add the oil and 2 cups of flour, and mix quickly with a strong spoon.
3. To make it fuzzy, add salt and the rest of the flour and mix it in.
4. By hand, fold and shape the dough into a ball that stays together. Cover it and set it aside. Fill the shells. Set a big Dutch oven over the fire and heat it up.
5. Spread a little olive oil on it, and then add the peppers, onions, and garlic.
6. Cook until the onion is clear. Take it off the heat.
7. When you add the lamb and spices, mix them together well (but don't turn on the heat).
8. Put it all together Separate the dough into two equal parts.
9. Roll out ½ of the dough into a big circle on a floured surface.
10. Place the dough on a cornmeal- or flour-dusted pizza peel or cutting board.
11. Cover the dough evenly with the filling, leaving about ¾" of space around the edge.
12. Clean your Dutch oven and put it over the fire to heat it up.
13. Then, roll out the rest of the dough into a round shape that looks like the first one.
14. Wet the edge of the bottom dough, then put the second half over the filling and dough, pressing to seal and rolling the edge under a little.
15. Put the pizza in the Dutch oven carefully, and then cover it.
16. Check every 20 minutes at first, then more often. It's done when the top crust is dry, and the bottom crust is golden brown.
17. Be careful to take it off the heat and the Dutch oven.

21. CHICKEN NOODLE SOUP

Prep Time: 5 Minutes | Cook Time: 35 Minutes

Total Time: 40 Minutes | Serving: 8

Ingredients

- 1/8 tsp black pepper plus more to taste
- 3 stalks celery
- 1/8 tsp onion powder
- 1/4 tsp Italian seasoning
- 1/8 tsp garlic powder
- 1/8 tsp kosher salt plus more to taste
- 1 pound boneless skinless chicken thighs
- 6 cups of chicken stock
- 1/2 large white onion
- 3 cloves garlic
- 4 large carrots
- 1 tbsp olive oil
- 2-3 cups of egg noodles

Instructions

1. Get all of the vegetables ready. Cut the carrots into thin rounds after peeling them. Cut the onion up. Small pieces of celery should be cut up. Cut up the garlic.
2. Set a big Dutch oven over medium heat on the stove. Put the onion and celery in the pot with the olive oil. Cook the vegetables for three to four minutes or until they begin to get soft.
3. This will make room for the chicken to cook. Move the onion and celery to the sides of the pot. If it needs it, add a little more olive oil to the bottom of the vessel. Season the chicken thighs with salt, onion powder, garlic powder, pepper, and Italian seasoning. Could you place them in the middle of the pot? It takes about two to three minutes on each side; cook the chicken until the outside is just barely clear.
4. Put the garlic, carrots, and chicken stock in the pot. Get rid of any brown bits on the pot's bottom. Set the soup on low heat and let it cook for 10 to 15 minutes or until the chicken is fully cooked.
5. Take the chicken out of the pot and put it on a plate or cutting board. Shred the chicken with two forks. The chicken and egg noodles should be put back in the pot. Let the soup simmer for another 8-10 minutes or until the noodles are cooked all the way through.
6. If you think the soup needs more salt and pepper, add it. Add fresh parsley to the soup, and enjoy!

22. HEALING CHICKEN NOODLE SOUP

Prep Time: 5 Minutes | Cook Time: 25 Minutes

Total Time: 30 Minutes | Serving: 6

Ingredients

- 8 cups of chicken broth or bone broth
- 1 bay leaf
- 4 medium carrots, peeled and sliced into ⅓rd inch rounds
- 2 cloves garlic, chopped
- 1 tbsp olive oil
- 2-3 cups of dry egg noodles I prefer flat noodles but you can use your preferred shape
- 1 medium onion, diced
- 2-3 tbsp chopped fresh parsley
- 1.5tsp salt
- 1 tsp turmeric
- 1 tsp fresh rosemary, chopped or sub ½ tsp dried rosemary
- 1 tsp fresh thyme leaves or sub ½ tsp dried thyme
- ½ lemon zest and juice
- pinch of cayenne optional
- ½ tsp black pepper
- 3 stalks celery, halved and sliced
- 1 rotisserie chicken, meat removed and shredded
- salt & pepper to taste

Instructions

1. While the heat is on medium to medium-high, swirl the olive oil around in a large Dutch oven or heavy kettle with a lid.
2. Put in the onion, carrots, and celery Saute on medium temperature for about 10 minutes until the vegetables get soft.
3. Salt, pepper, cayenne pepper, rosemary, thyme, garlic, and lemon zest should be added. For about one to two minutes, or until the garlic smells good, saute over medium-low heat.
4. Add one bay leaf and the juice of half a lemon as you pour in the chicken or bone broth. Over medium-high heat, stir everything and bring to a boil.
5. Add 2 to 3 cups of egg noodles and chicken shreds when it starts to boil. Bring it back to a boil, then cover it and lower the heat.
6. Let the pasta cook slowly over low heat for 10 to 15 minutes or until it is soft. Take it off the heat. Feel free to taste and add more salt and pepper if you like. Serve with chopped parsley on top. Enjoy!

23. HOT ITALIAN SAUSAGE SOUP

Prep Time: 30 Minutes | Cook Time: 50 Minutes

Total Time: 1 Hour 20 Minutes | Serving: 8

Ingredients

- 6 medium sized potatoes cubed to rustic bite-sized pieces
- 1 cup of heavy cream
- 1 pound bulk hot Italian sausage
- 4 cloves garlic minced
- Salt to taste at serving

- 4 slices bacon diced in 1/2 inch pieces
- 2 cups of packed fresh spinach stems removed
- 1 medium onion diced
- Black pepper to taste at serving
- 2 (32 ounce) cartons chicken broth

Instructions

1. Heat up the campfire to medium-low levels and start cooking.
2. Hang your Dutch oven over the fire with a Dutch Oven Tripod if you don't have a campfire grill grate. This Hot Italian Sausage Soup Campfire Recipe will still work.
3. Brown the sausage in a 12-inch DEEP camp Dutch oven (not the regular depth oven; this is the size for soups and stews) until it's no longer pink. Use a wooden spoon to break it up as it cooks. Take the crumbled meat out and cover a plate with paper towels.
4. If the Dutch oven has a lot of grease, take most of it out. If your sausage is pretty lean, you don't need to take out the grease.
5. The bacon should now be added to the Dutch oven and cooked until it is crispy. Similarly, if there is a lot of grease, take some of it off... The Dutch oven needs to have a fair amount of oil on the bottom so that the onions and garlic can cook.
6. Add the onions and garlic just before the bacon starts to get crispy. Saute them until they soften. Bring the chicken broth to a boil after adding it.
7. Get the campfire very hot, and if you need to, add more wood. Cover the soup pot with a lid to help the water boil faster.
8. Now take off the lid of the cast iron pot and add the cubed potatoes. Put the lid back on top and cook for another minute. Bring the soup back to a boil and cook the vegetables until they are soft.
9. Add the hot Italian sausage and heavy cream back to the pot when the potato chunks are soft. Keep cooking on low heat with the lid off of the pot until the ingredients are warm all the way through and the soup gets a little thicker.
10. Before serving, put the fresh spinach and stir it in. Then, use a ladle to pour the sausage and potato soup into strong bowls.

24. SAUSAGE AND BEAN CASSEROLE

Prep Time: 10 Minutes | Cook Time: 1 Hour 30 Minutes

Total Time: 1 Hour 40 Minutes | Serving: 8

Ingredients

- 1 celery stalk chopped
- 400g diced tomatoes 14 ounce
- 5 mushrooms chopped
- 1 L beef stock 33 fl ounce
- 1 onion chopped
- 1 tbsp vegetable oil
- 2-4 slices bacon chopped

- 600g baked beans 21 ounce (1 big tin, or two small tins), use ham sauce or bbq sauce for extra flavour
- 2 cloves garlic
- 2 carrots chopped
- 6 sausages cooked and chopped – leftover bbq sausages work great
- 3 potatoes medium size, chopped

Instructions

1. In a deep pan, like a remoska or camp oven, heat the vegetable oil.
2. A tbsp of oil
3. The sausages should be cooked on high for about 10 to 15 minutes. If you are using leftovers, skip this step.
4. 6 hams
5. Put in the garlic and onions, and cook until the onions are clear. After you add the bacon, cook for three more minutes or until the bacon is almost done.
6. 2 cloves of garlic, 1 onion, and 4 to 6 bacon slices
7. Add the chopped potatoes, carrots, and celery, and mix them quickly. Add the cooked sausages and mushrooms, and stir them in slowly so they don't break.
8. 1 stalk of celery, 2 carrots, 3 potatoes, 5 mushrooms
9. Bring it to a boil after adding the beef stock. Set the pot on low heat and cover it for 30 minutes. If cooking over a campfire, move the pot away from the coals to lower the heat. Every 5 to 10 minutes, stir the food to make sure nothing falls to the bottom.
10. 1 liter of beef broth
11. You should make sure the potato is fully cooked before adding the diced tomatoes and baked beans. Blend everything together well. Turn down the heat and leave the lid off for another 15 to 30 minutes after it starts to boil again. Now is the time to add the cornstarch slurry and mix it in. This will make the casserole thicker.
12. 600 g baked beans, 400 g diced tomatoes and 2 tbsp of cornstarch or cornflour
13. Serve right away while still hot. Add some salt and pepper on top, and then dip it in a big piece of damper or crusty bread. Add some salt and pepper.

25. BEEF STEW

Prep Time: 15 Minutes | Cook Time: 1 Hour 30 Minutes | Additional Time: 15 Minutes

Total Time: 2 Hour | Serving: 8

Ingredients

- 2 tbsp Worcestershire sauce
- 2 tbsp butter or olive oil
- 1½ cups of thawed frozen peas
- 2 cups of mushrooms
- 2 bay leaves
- ½ cup of chopped fresh parsley
- 6 ounce can of tomato paste
- 4 medium potatoes
- 3 ribs of celery
- ⅛ tsp. ground thyme
- 2 medium onions

- 1 tsp Paprika
- 1½ tsp Ground rosemary
- 6 cups of cold water or beef stock
- 4-6 cloves of minced garlic
- ¼ cup of flour
- ¼ tsp. oregano
- 1 pound stew meat
- 4 carrots
- salt & pepper
- optional: jalapeno pepper or hot sauce

Instructions

1. Cut the meat into pieces that are ½" thick. Cut up the potatoes, onion, celery, mushrooms, carrots, and onion.
2. Set up a Dutch oven over the campfire to get it hot.In the pot, melt the butter or olive oil.
3. When you add the meat chunks, stir them in and cook until they turn gray.
4. Put the flour in. Make sure not to burn the flour as you stir it all the time until it turns brown. Slowly add ½ cup of cold water or beef broth while stirring all the time. Do not stop the boiling process.Don't add more than ½ to 1 cup at a time, because adding cold water to a hot cast iron pot can break the iron.
5. Cut up the onion, carrot, and celery and add them to the pot. For about 10 minutes, stir the food often. It will not stick if you add small amounts of water or broth.
6. Place the garlic and mushrooms in the bowl. For 5 minutes, stir and cook.
7. Put in the tomato paste, Worcestershire sauce or red wine, spices, and the rest of the broth or water. Put a lid on top when it starts to boil.
8. Bring the heat down to a simmer. To do this, we take it out of the campfire and heat it with coals. Stir every now and then for 45 minutes.
9. Take off the lid and add the frozen peas. Put the lid back on and cook for another 15 minutes. You can put salt or pepper to the stew based on your taste.
10. Add chopped fresh parsley and serve. People who like things a little spicy can add some chopped Jalapenos or hot sauce.

26. JACKFRUIT VEGGIE SOUP

Prep Time: 20 Minutes | Cook Time: 1 Hour | Total Time: 1 Hour 30 Minutes | Serving: 8

Ingredients

- green beans
- bay leaf
- garlic
- mushrooms
- diced tomatoes
- salt & pepper
- carrots
- potato
- water
- soy sauce
- thyme
- celery
- green jackfruit
- vegan vegetable bullion
- red pepper flakes
- onion
- sweet potato
- parsnip

Instructions

1. Peel the veggies and cut them up.
2. Put the bullion and water in the Dutch oven to make the vegetable stock.
3. Put everything into a pot and heat it over the campfire.
4. Put the lid on the pot and cook for about 45 to 70 minutes, or until the vegetables are soft.

27. VEGETABLE STEW

Prep Time: 5 Minutes | Cook Time: 25 Minutes | Total Time: 30 Minutes | Serving: 4

Ingredients

- 8 ounce mushrooms, halved or quartered
- 8-10 baby potatoes, cubed
- 1 tbsp tomato paste
- 1 tbsp liquid aminos, or soy sauce
- 1 tsp salt
- 1 tsp thyme
- 2 cups of vegetable stock
- ½ cup of red wine
- 2 tbsp flour
- 1 small onion, chopped
- 1 bay leaf
- 2 cloves garlic, minced
- 2 large carrots, sliced
- 2 tbsp oil
- 1 celery stick, sliced

Instructions

1. In a big pot, heat up 1 tbsp of oil. Put in the mushrooms and cook for about 5 minutes, until they turn brown. Put in the potatoes, onion, carrot, celery, and salt. Saute for two to three minutes. After you add the tomato paste and garlic, cook for one more minute.
2. Putting in the flour. Put the vegetables in the flour and stir them around. Then put the red wine and liquid aminos or soy sauce.
3. Keep cooking until almost all of the red wine is gone. Put in the bay leaf, thyme, and vegetable stock. Put a lid on top and simmer for 10 minutes. After that, take the lid off and let the stew thicken for another 10 minutes. Check the seasonings and divide the vegetables between bowls once they are soft. Enjoy!

28. SMOKY POTATO BACON CORN CHOWDER

Prep Time: 15 Minutes | Cook Time: 1 Minutes

Total Time: 1 Hour 15 Minutes | Serving: 8

Ingredients

- 2 bay leaves
- 4 stalks of celery medium diced
- 1 bottle of your favorite beer
- pepper
- 1 liter 35% cream
- 2 carrots medium diced
- 1 liter chicken stock
- salt
- 5 sprigs of thyme
- 3 cups of diced baby red potatoes
- 4 ears of fresh corn
- 1 red onion small diced
- 3 cloves of garlic
- ½ pound of thick sliced bacon

Instructions

1. First, render the bacon. This will give you the grease you need to saute the vegetables.
2. Dice the onion, garlic, celery, and carrot and add them. Give the veggies two minutes to cook while you stir them.
3. While the pot is cooking, cut the corn off the cob and dice the potatoes.
4. When the food is soft, add the corn and potatoes to the pot.
5. Use the beer to clean out the pot, then add the chicken stock, herbs, and cream.
6. Keep the pot on low heat until the potatoes are done and the liquid starts to get a little less. and the chowder has become a little thicker.
7. Add salt and pepper to taste.

29. CHICKEN STEW

Prep Time: 5 Minutes | Cook Time: 2 Hour

Total Time: 2 Hour 5 Minutes | Serving: 6

Ingredients

- 2 pounds chicken breast
- 3 celery stalks sliced
- 2 Tbsp tomato paste
- ⅛ tsp cayenne red pepper
- 1/2 tsp black pepper plus more to taste at end
- 2 Tbsp vegetable oil
- ¼ cup of flour
- 1/2 tsp salt plus more to taste at end
- 1 pound gold potatoes cut into 1 inch chunks
- 2 cloves garlic minced
- 2 bay leaves
- 3 large carrots trimmed and sliced
- 1 tsp dried thyme
- 4 cups of chicken stock
- 12 ounces pearl onions or 1.5 cups of diced yellow onion

Instructions

1. Put the chicken in a bag with 1/2 tsp, 1/2 tsp of salt, and 2 tbsp of oil of black pepper. Cut the chicken into big chunks that are easy to bite.
2. Whisk the flour and about 1/4 cup of the stock together until they form a slurry. This is the roux.
3. Get the vegetables ready and put them in a gallon-sized bag. Add the roux and the rest of the ingredients to the vegetable bag.
4. Put the Dutch oven on the fire in an area with a lot of heat when you're ready to cook. Make it hot. Put in the chicken and cook for about 10 minutes, or until it gets some color and is mostly done.
5. Set the pot over the stove to a medium level of heat. Put the vegetable bag in with the rest of the food. Cover, stir, and cook for an hour and a half to two hours. Keep it at a simmer and stir it every so often to keep it from sticking. Make any necessary changes to the pot over the heat source to keep the temperature at a medium or medium-low level. Add salt and pepper to taste. Serve hot with bread to dip it in.

30. FISH LENTIL STEW

Prep Time: 5 Minutes | Cook Time: 25 Minutes

Total Time: 30 Minutes | Serving: 4

Ingredients

- 2 tsp garam masala
- 1 cup of red lentils (rinsed and sorted)
- 12 ounces white fish (2 large or 3-4 small fillets) Cod, halibut, sablefish, grouper or lingcod will work well
- 1 tsp salt
- 1 onion, diced
- 1 tsp garlic powder
- 3 ½ cups of water
- 15 ounce can diced tomatoes
- 1 tbsp olive oil
- 1 15 ounce can spinach, drained Or use -2 ounces fresh or -10 ounces frozen spinach.

Instructions

1. Prepare campfire: Get the coals very hot or let a campfire burn out until the wood is smoldering but there are no more flames.
2. Put onions, salt, garlic, spices, olive oil, and more into the Dutch oven. Put out in the open on coals. Wait one to two minutes for the onions to get soft.
3. Place the tomatoes in the pot and cook for two to three minutes, until the tomatoes start to boil.
4. Put in the lentils, spinach, and water. Bring the mix to a boil. Put the fish in the pot.
5. For about 15 minutes, or until the lentils are soft and the fish is opaque and flaky, cover the Dutch oven and cook. You might need to cook the fish for another 5 to 10 minutes, depending on how thick it is.
6. Let the lentils cool down a bit before you serve them.

31. COWBOY STEW

Prep Time: 5 Minutes | Cook Time: 1 Hour 30 Minutes

Total Time: 1 Hour 35 Minutes | Serving: 6

Ingredients

- 1 (15 ounce can) cut green beans, undrained
- 1 (4 ounce can) chopped green chilies
- 1 pound ground beef
- 1/4 tsp black pepper
- 1 (15 ounce can) pinto beans, undrained
- 3 tbsp all-purpose flour
- 1 (15 ounce can) whole kernel corn, undrained
- 2 slices thick bacon chopped into 1/4 inch pieces
- 1 (14 ounce package) hot smoked andouille sausage, sliced into 1/2 inch pieces
- 1 (15 ounce can) diced tomatoes, undrained
- 4 garlic cloves minced
- 1 medium onion chopped
- 4 medium potatoes peeled and cubed into 1/2 inch pieces
- 1/2 tsp salt

Instructions

1. You can use campfire coals, charcoal briquettes, a camp stove, or an RV stove to heat up a 12-inch cast iron Dutch oven over medium heat.
2. When you add the bacon, stir it in and cook until it gets a little brown. Do not take the fat out of the pot. Put the onion and garlic in the pot and stir them around until they get soft.
3. Put in the ground beef. As it browns, use a spoon to break it up into crumbles. Do not take the fat out of the pot. When you add the sausage, cook it until it's just warmed up, stirring every now and then.
4. Now add the flour, salt, and pepper to the pot and mix them together. Make sure the flour is fully mixed in, and cook it for a few minutes before adding the rest of the ingredients.
5. Put in the corn, beans, tomatoes, green chilies, and potatoes. Using a whisk to mix all the items together. Bring to a boil, then lower the tempreature and simmer. Cook with the lid on for about an hour, stirring every now and then to make sure nothing sticks to the bottom of the pot.

32. NO KNEAD DUTCH OVEN BREAD

Prep Time: 10 Minutes | Cook Time: 40 Minutes

Total Time: 50 Minutes | Serving: 6

Ingredients

- ➤ 2 tsp flaked sea salt OR 1 3/4 tsp table salt
- ➤ 3 cups of all purpose flour
- ➤ 1 tsp active dry yeast
- ➤ 1 1/2 cups of warm water

Instructions

1. Put the flour and salt in a big bowl and stir to mix. Mix the yeast and water into the flour with a spoon until a sticky batter forms, and there are no more bits of raw flour. Here is where you would add the cheese or herbs and mix them in.
2. After 18 to 24 hours, cover with plastic wrap and leave alone. To make the dough more than double in size and full of tiny bubbles.
3. When you're ready to bake, heat up your 5 quart (or smaller) cast iron pot and its lid in the oven with the heat on 450. Set it on high for 20 to 30 minutes.
4. The pot is ready when you take it out of the oven and set it aside. Somewhat coat the dough in flour—about a tbsp—and make sure your hands are very floured. Punch the dough right through the middle with your fist to make it flat. Next, gently roll the dough into a ball. You can flour your hands if you need to, but don't add any more flour to the dough. There will still be stickiness. No problem.
5. Cover the bottom of your pot with one more tbsp of flour, and then put the dough in it. Cover with the lid and cook for 30 minutes. Take off the lid and bake for another ten minutes. Put on a wire rack to cool.

33. DUTCH OVEN POTATOES

Prep Time: 20 Minutes | Cook Time: 45 Minutes | Total Time: 1 Hour 5 Minutes | Serving: 6

Ingredients

For the Potatoes:

- 8 medium sized potatoes red, yukon gold, or russet, sliced thin
- 2 1/2 cups of cheese cheddar, Monterey jack, or pepper jack
- 1 jalapeno seeds and membranes removed, diced
- 1 tsp season salt
- 1 medium onion diced
- 1/2 pound bacon diced

Dutch Oven:

- 12 inch shallow dutch oven
- 27-30 coals lit and heated until beginning to turn grey.

Instructions

1. The bacon should be cooked over about half of the coals until it is chewy. It will get good and crispy while the potatoes cook.
2. Get the Dutch oven off the coals and take out the bacon and any extra grease. In the bottom of the oven, leave about 2 tbsp of bacon fat.
3. In the bottom of the Dutch oven, put half of the sliced potatoes and sprinkle with half a tsp of season salt. Place half of the onion, half of the bacon, and then half of the cheese on top of the potatoes. You can also add half of the Jalapeno if you want.
4. Add more layers with the rest of the ingredients, and then cover the Dutch oven with the lid.

For the Baking with Coals:

1. Put the Dutch oven on a stand or a safe spot on the ground. Then, put 9 coals on the bottom and 18 coals on top. For a 12-inch shallow Dutch oven, this should heat up to about 375 degrees. Check on the coals occasionally and add more when the ones already there start to die down.
2. The bottom of the potatoes may be cooking too quickly, even after adjusting the coals. To fix this, add 1/3 cup of water to the bottom of the Dutch oven.
3. After about 45 minutes, the potatoes are done when they are soft.

For Baking in the Oven:

1. Heat an oven to 400°F and put the food in it.
2. Put the potatoes in the oven and bake for fifty to sixty minutes, or until they are soft. To see if this is true, put a fork or butter knife in the middle of the potatoes.

34. CAMPING MAC AND CHEESE

Prep Time: 30 Minutes | Cook Time: 30 Minutes | Additional Time: 10 Minutes

Total Time: 1 Hour 10 Minutes | Serving: 8

Ingredients

- 1 jar of alfredo sauce, 15 ounce
- 1 cup of milk
- 1 pound of shredded sharp cheddar cheese
- 1 pound of shredded pizza cheese
- 1 box of elbow macaroni, 32 ounce
- optional: your favorite potato chips

Instructions

1. Lighting and getting 20 or more pieces of charcoal ready will help heat up your Dutch oven. Follow the instruction on the package to cook the macaroni.
2. After draining the macaroni, put it in the Dutch oven.
3. Add the whole jar of Alfredo sauce and mix it in. Incorporate the milk cup.
4. Pour in half of the pizza cheese shreds and mix them in. It'll be easier to mix it evenly if you add half at a time. Combine the rest of the bag with the first part.
5. Using cheddar cheese, do the same thing as the half-and-half.
6. Available but not required: Add several handfuls of broken up potato chips on top of the noodles. Secure the Dutch oven's lid.
7. Line up eight charcoal pieces in a circle. Set the iron oven on top of the circle.
8. On top of the Dutch oven's lid, spread out 12 pieces of charcoal.
9. For 30 to 40 minutes, or until the cheese melts and the sauce is the right consistency for you, bake the macaroni casserole. Serving right away.

35. POTATOES AU GRATIN

Prep Time: 20 Minutes | Cook Time: 1 Hour 15 Minutes

Total Time: 1 Hour 35 Minutes | Serving: 8

Ingredients

- 4 cloves garlic minced
- 1 (14 ounce) can chicken broth
- 2 tsp cornstarch
- 3 cups of shredded sharp cheddar cheese
- 5 large Idaho or russet potatoes about 3 pounds, scrubbed and sliced 1/8 to 1/4 inch thick (use a sharp knife or mandolin for easy slicing and uniform sized pieces)
- 1/2 cup of grated Parmesan cheese
- 1 pound bacon cut into 1/4 inch pieces
- 1/2 cup of heavy cream
- 1 tsp dried thyme
- Salt to taste
- 1 small onion sliced thin
- Black pepper to taste

Instructions

1. As directed, prepare the ingredients.
2. Charcoal briquettes should be ready to be baked at 400 degrees F. There are 29 coals needed. Heat a standard-depth 12-inch cast iron Dutch oven with bottom coals only. Fry bacon until it is crispy.
3. Mix the heavy cream, garlic, cornstarch, thyme, chicken broth, salt, and black pepper in a medium bowl with a whisk while the bacon is cooking. Set the bowl aside.
4. Place the bacon on a paper towel or tissue paper to drain.
5. Add half of the potatoes, all of the onion slices, half of the bacon, and a third of the cheddar cheese to the pot. Do not drain the grease from the pan.
6. Put in another layer of the rest of the potatoes and bacon.
7. Mix the cream with the liquid that you set aside, and then pour it over the potatoes.
8. Cover the whole dish with the rest of the cheddar cheese and all of the Parmesan cheese.
9. Place 29 coals (nine on top of the lid and ten below the bottom of the oven) and cover with the lid. Bake at 400 degrees F.
10. It will take about an hour of baking until the potatoes are soft and the top is golden brown. Allow to cool for ten minutes after taking from the heat.

36. CORNBREAD CHILI

Prep Time: 15 Minutes | Cook Time: 45 Minutes

Total Time: 1 Hour | Serving: 8

Ingredients

- 1 anaheim chile, seeded & diced
- 1 tsp cumin
- 1 box of cornbread mix
- 1 tbsp extra virgin olive oil
- ½ tsp salt
- 4 garlic cloves, minced
- 2 tbsp chile powder
- 1 red bell pepper, seeded & diced
- 15 ounce canned tomato sauce
- 3 ounce chipotle chile in adobo sauce

- 1 ½ pound ground turkey
- 15 ounce canned black beans, drained an rinsed
- 1 Jalapeno pepper, seeded & diced
- ½ cup of water, if needed
- 15 ounce canned diced tomatoes
- 1 onion, diced
- 4 ounce green chiles, canned, drained & diced

Instructions

1. Add 35 charcoal briquettes to a fire ring or some other item that can't catch fire.
2. Light the briquettes and let them heat up for twenty to thirty minutes.
3. Put a 10-inch cast iron Dutch oven on top of the hot coals when the flames are out.
4. Put olive oil in the Dutch oven.
5. Diced onions, bell peppers, anaheim chile, and Jalapeno pepper should be added and mixed in. It will take about 5 minutes of cooking until the vegetables start to get soft.
6. In a pan, add the vegetables and ground turkey. Cook until the meat is mostly browned.
7. Put salt, cumin, and chili powder to taste.
8. Add the diced tomatoes, beans, tomato sauce, chipotle chile, and green chiles from a can. You might need more water if your coals are too hot.
9. Chili should be left to cook on low heat for at least 30 minutes and up to several hours. Your chili will taste better if you let it cook for longer. Take out 10 to 15 coals from under the Dutch oven if you are going to let the chili cook for hours. While it's cooking, keep an eye on the coals and the heat. If the old coals run out, you might need to add more.
10. Mix them together. One box of cornbread mix. For some brands, all you need to do is add water. Add cornbread batter to the top of your chili and spread it out evenly.
11. Place about 16 hot coals on top of the lid and cover the Dutch oven.
12. It should take about 20 to 30 minutes for the cornbread to brown and be done while the chili cooks.

37. PASTA MARINARA

Prep Time: 5 Minutes | Cook Time: 25 Minutes

Total Time: 30 Minutes | Serving: 4

Ingredients

- 1 tsp Italian herb mix
- 1 tsp garlic powder
- 28 ounce jar marinara sauce (pasta sauce)
- 14 ounce can diced tomatoes
- 2 cups of vegetable broth
- 1 pound short-grain pasta Use gluten-free pasta if necessary, such as Banza
- 1 small red onion, diced
- 1 cup of water
- 1 tbsp oil
- 2 sweet bell peppers (diced, seeds + membranes removed) Or 6 mini sweet peppers
- ½ tsp red pepper flakes (optional)

Instructions

Prepare campfire:

1. Get the coals very hot or let a campfire burn out until the wood is smoldering but there are no more flames.
2. In a Dutch oven, put salt, pepper, garlic, herbs, red pepper flakes, and diced onion. Leave the oven open on the coals. It will take about three minutes of cooking until the onions start to sizzle.
3. After you add the diced tomatoes, cook for about one minute or until the liquid starts to boil. Put in the tomato sauce and broth. Bring up the temperature.
4. Could you put in the pasta and mix it in? Make sure there is enough water to cover the pasta. If necessary, add more broth or water.
5. Let the pasta cook in the broth until it's soft and most of the broth is absorbed. This could take up to 15 minutes, based on the type of pasta and how hot your campfire is. Make sure to scrape the bottom of the pot often while the pasta is cooking so that it doesn't stick.
6. It means the pasta is sticking to the pot if you hear sizzling. Add a little more water and stir the pasta to get rid of any stuck pieces.
7. Take the pasta off the heat when it's soft. Add a little more water and stir the pasta if it looks dry. Serve right away.

38. EASY PANZANELLA SALAD

Prep Time: 10 Minutes | Cook Time: 10 Minutes

Total Time: 20 Minutes | Serving: 4

Ingredients

- ➢ 1 yellow,green, or orange sweet pepper, chopped
- ➢ 1/2 red onion, diced
- ➢ 1/4 tsp freshly ground black pepper
- ➢ 4 cups of stale french bread, cut into cubes
- ➢ 3 ounce. fresh mozzarella or feta cheese, cubed
- ➢ 1/4 tsp kosher salt
- ➢ 1 large tomato, chopped, or 1 cup of halved cherry tomatoes
- ➢ 3 tbsp white wine vinegar
- ➢ 1 tsp finely minced garlic

For the vinaigrette:

- ➢ 1 Tbsp olive oil
- ➢ 1/2 tsp kosher salt
- ➢ 1 tsp Dijon mustard
- ➢ 1/4 cup of olive oil
- ➢ 1 cucumber, chopped

Instructions

1. On a camp stove or over a fire, heat 1 tbsp of oil over medium-low temperature. Add the bread cubes and 1/2 tsp of salt. Cook, stirring every so often, until the bread is nicely browned. If you need to, add more oil.
2. Take the pepper, red onion, tomatoes, and cucumbers and cut them up. Put them in a large bowl. Add pepper and salt.
3. Put the bread cubes in the bowl with the vegetables.
4. Pour the vinaigrette over your salad after shaking it up. Add more salt and pepper to taste. Stir everything together until it's well mixed.
5. You can serve the salad right away, or let it sit at room temperature for 30 minutes while you grill some sausages. These steps will help the tastes mix a little.

39. BAKED BEANS

Prep Time: 10 Minutes | Cook Time: 1 Hour 30 Minutes

Total Time: 1 Hour 40 Minutes | Serving: 12

Ingredients

- 1/2 cup of yellow mustard
- 1 tsp black pepper
- 3 garlic cloves minced
- 1/4 cup of vinegar
- 1 pound bacon chopped in 1-inch pieces
- 1/4 tsp cayenne pepper
- 1/4 cup of molasses
- 1/2 cup of brown sugar
- 1 cup of ketchup
- 1 medium onion chopped
- 2 tsp salt
- 1 pound ground beef
- 1 (16 ounce) can lima beans (undrained)
- 1 (16 ounce) can butter beans
- 1 (16 ounce) can great northern beans
- 1 (16 ounce) can pinto beans (undrained)
- 1 (16 ounce) can red kidney beans (undrained)

Instructions

1. As directed, prepare the ingredients.
2. Warm up a cast iron Dutch oven with a depth of 12 inches or a standard depth of 14 inches.
3. Browning the bacon in the pot will take about 15 minutes of bottom-only medium-high heat. Put the oven's lid on top to keep the heat in if the bacon isn't browning fast enough. Add the ground beef to the pot when the bacon is fully browned. As the meat browns, about 10 minutes, use a spoon to break it up.
4. Before you serve the meat, use a tissue paper to soak up most of the grease, but not all of it. Put the garlic and onion in the pot and stir them with the meat.
5. Add the rest of the ingredients to the pot and stir them together once the vegetables are soft. Please remember not to drain the beans. They will give you flavor and liquid, so you shouldn't need to add water or broth.
6. Set up the 23 charcoals for baking at 325 degrees F, with 16 on top of the lid and 7 below the bottom of the oven. Place the lid on top of the oven and turn it on.
7. While the beans are baking, stir the pot about every 20 minutes.
8. After about 60 to 90 minutes, the beans are done when most of the liquid has been soaked up and the sauce is thick and a deep golden brown color. Take off the lid and put all the coals under the oven if the sauce is too thin. Keep the pot on low heat and stir it every so often to make sure nothing sticks to the bottom. Let the sauce thicken to your liking.

41. CAMPFIRE CORN ON THE COB

Prep Time: 5 Minutes | Cook Time: 30 Minutes | Additional Time: 30

Total Time: 1 Hour 5 Minutes | Serving: 4

Ingredients

- ➢ 8 Ears of sweet corn
- ➢ Butter
- ➢ Water for soaking about 2 gallons
- ➢ Salt & Pepper

Instructions

1. Pull back the top layer of husks to get the silk off of the corn. Wrap the corn in the husks again.
2. Put your ears completely under cold water and soak for about 30 minutes. In order to keep the cobs under water, you might need to put a lid or pan over them. If you don't, they'll likely float to the top.
3. While the corn is soaking, get your cooking source ready. For example, a campfire with coals, charcoal briquettes, or a propane grill set to 350°F for medium heat.
4. If you want to know if your heat source is about 350°F degrees, you don't need a thermometer. Just use your hand (make sure nothing is on it that could catch fire, like jewelry or clothes).
5. Hold your hand's palm about 5 inches above the heat source.
6. Now take your hand off the heat before it hurts and write down the time.
7. Medium heat for 5 to 7 seconds. Take the extra water out of the corn.
8. Corn should be grilled over medium heat, turning it about every 5 minutes, for about 30 minutes, or until it is soft.
9. Wearing gloves will help you avoid getting burned as you carefully pull back the husks. There will be a light char on the kernels. If you want a stronger charred flavor, put the cobs back over the hot coals until they are charred the way you like them.
10. If you wish, you can add butter, salt, and pepper on top.

42. PINTO BEANS

Prep Time: 10 Minutes | Cook Time: 1 Hour 30 Minutes |Total Time: 1 Hour 40 Minutes
Serving: 9

Ingredients

- 1 pound smoked pork hocks
- 2 tbsp oil
- 1 pound dried pinto beans
- 1/2 cup of green chiles
- 1/8 tsp ground cayenne pepper
- 2 dried bay leaves

- 4 cloves garlic
- 1 large yellow onion
- 1 tsp freshly ground black pepper
- 2 quarts chicken stock
- kosher salt

Instructions

The Night Before:

1. Sort through the dried beans to get rid of any rocks or other things in them. Putting the beans in a big bowl and adding enough water to cover them by at least 2 inches comes next.
2. Roast the green chiles. To get the skins completely black, roast the green chiles over charcoal, a gas burner, or on the top rack of your oven under the broiler. Wrap it in plastic wrap and put it in a bowl. Wait for it to cool. Take off the skins and pat them dry with your fingers. Take off the stems and seeds, and then cut them into small pieces.

The Next Day:

1. Wash and drain your beans. Light 18 briquettes of charcoal in a chimney starter or grill pit. If the coals are white, they are ready to be put under your cast iron Dutch oven. Make sure they are evenly spaced. Put the cooking oil in the Dutch oven and heat it until it shimmers. Put in the diced onions and cook them until they become clear and start to turn brown. Fill the pot with chicken stock, beans, pork hocks, garlic, bay leaves, cayenne pepper, and black pepper. Give it a good stir. Put a lid on it and boil it.
2. When the pot starts to boil, take out enough charcoal to leave about 8–10 under the Dutch oven. This will bring the pot down to a simmer. Simmer with the lid on for an hour, adding new coals every 30 minutes or so to keep the simmer going.
3. Move the pork hocks to a cutting board from the beans. Take the meat and skin off the bones. Throw away the skin and bones Cut the meat into small pieces and add them back to the pot. Dice the green chiles and add them to the pot. Then, smash about half a cup of the beans against the side of the pot and add them back in. This will make the broth creamy. Put the lid on top and cook on low heat for another 30 minutes or until the beans are soft. Add more stock if the broth looks like it's too thick. If it's too thin, put enough hot coals under it to bring it back to a boil. Then, take the lid off and let it reduce until it's the right consistency. Serve with salt to taste.

43. CHEESY CAMPFIRE POTATOES

Prep Time: 15 Minutes | Cook Time: 40 Minutes

Total Time: 55 Minutes | Serving: 4

Ingredients

- ➢ 1 tbsp olive oil
- ➢ 1 onion thinly sliced
- ➢ 1 clove garlic minced
- ➢ 1 pound baby potatoes halved or quartered into ½ inch pieces
- ➢ ¼ cup of chicken broth
- ➢ 2 tbsp fresh parsley chopped
- ➢ 2 tbsp butter diced
- ➢ ¼ cup of shredded cheddar cheese
- ➢ salt and pepper to taste

Instructions

Prep foil packet:

1. Overlay two long, thick pieces of heavy-duty aluminum foil on top of each other to make a cross.
2. The potatoes and onion should be in the middle of the foil. Put garlic, parsley, cheese, butter, salt, and pepper on top, and then drizzle with olive oil. Take care and use clean hands to toss the potatoes to coat them.
3. Spread the potatoes out in a "bowl" made of folded-up foil. Add chicken broth and seal the pouch well.

Cook foil packet:

1. Over medium heat, cook potatoes in foil on a grill or fire for 30 to 40 minutes or until they are soft. Bake in a foil packet at 425°F for 30 to 35 minutes or until done.
2. When you open the packets, be careful not to let the hot steam out.

44. CAMPFIRE MUSHROOMS

Prep Time: 15 Minutes | Cook Time: 15 Minutes

Total Time: 30 Minutes | Serving: 4

Ingredients

- 2 tbsp olive oil
- 2 cloves garlic, minced
- 3 tbsp butter
- 1/4 pound morels or other wild mushrooms of choice, cleans and ends cut off
- 1 pound brown cremini mushrooms, cleaned and cut into thirds
- 3 small sprigs fresh rosemary
- 1/4 pound shiitake mushrooms, cleaned and cut into thick slices
- 2 small shallots, minced
- 1/4 cup of red or white wine or stock or water
- 1/2 lemon, optional,

Instructions

1. Use wood to start your campfire. The smoke will give your mushroom dish more depth.
2. Put a cooking grate on the fire once the coals are ready.
3. Place a big pan that can handle the heat on top.
4. Mix in the butter and olive oil until the butter melts.
5. Make a stir and add the shallots. Cook for one minute.
6. Put in the rosemary and garlic and mix it in.
7. Stir in the brown cremini mushrooms and cook for three to five minutes, until they get a little soft. It will depend on how hot the fire is how long it takes to cook.
8. Put in the shiitake mushrooms, stir them in, and cook for another three to five minutes.
9. If you want to use lemon juice, add it and stir it in. Cook for one minute.
10. You can use water, stock, or wine. Cook for about 5 minutes to turn down the heat.
11. Add morels or other soft wild mushrooms and stir them in. Heat the mixture slowly for three minutes. Serve on top of chicken or steak that has been grilled.

45.CORNBREAD

Prep Time: 5 Minutes | Cook Time: 30 Minutes | Resting Time: 5 Minutes

Total Time: 40 Minutes | Serving: 8

Ingredients

- 1/2 tsp baking soda
- 1 tbsp sugar
- 2 cups of cornmeal
- 1 tsp salt
- 1 cup of buttermilk

- 2 large eggs beaten
- 2 tsp baking powder
- 1 (15 ounce) can cream style corn
- 2 tbsp butter

Optional for serving:

- Butter if desired

- Honey or jam for sweetness if desired

Instructions

1. Complete the steps for the ingredients.
2. Measuring and mixing dry ingredients marked with an asterisk at home is possible.
3. Bring a 10-inch Dutch oven with a standard depth of 350 degrees F. Place 21 briquettes or uniform campfire coals on top of the lid and 7 below the bottom of the oven to heat it. A cast iron skillet or nonstick baking pan works well for baking in a propane camp oven, regular oven, or RV oven. Apply butter or nonstick spray to the cast iron pan to make cleaning easier.
1. Measure out 1 cup of buttermilk. NOTE: You can use one cup of milk and a tbsp of vinegar instead of buttermilk. Let it sit for five minutes, and then continue with the recipe.
4. Mix the eggs, buttermilk, and corn in a medium-sized bowl using a whisk.
5. Add the baking powder, sugar, baking soda, salt, and cornmeal to the bowl and mix until everything is combined.
6. Set the Dutch oven on high heat and add the butter. Let it melt. Camping Food The bread will be easier to remove from the Dutch oven if you line it with parchment paper. However, I like the bottom of this cornbread recipe to be crispier, so I bake it in the bottom of the prepared pan with the liquid butter. You can use parchment paper to line a Dutch oven. Find out how to use Dutch oven liners at campingforfoodies.com.
7. I was putting the batter in the oven and covering it with the lid. Set up 7 coals below the oven and 14 on the lid for baking.
8. If you want the baking to be even, turn the oven and lid around every 10 minutes.
9. It will take about 30 minutes of baking until the bread is golden brown and a toothpick stuck in the middle comes out clean.
10. Take the meat off the heat and let it cool down a bit. Then, cut it up and serve.
11. If you want, you can spread it with butter and then drizzle it with honey or jam.

46. STUFFED PEPPERS

Prep Time: 30 Minutes | Cook Time: 30 Minutes

Total Time: 1 Hour | Serving: 6

Ingredients

- 3/4 cup of shredded extra sharp cheddar
- 2 cloves garlic, minced
- 1 large onion, chopped
- 1 15-ounce can tomato sauce
- 2 tbsp ketchup
- 6 bell peppers
- 14 ounces vegetarian ground meat (or real meat, if you like)
- 10 ounces mushrooms, chopped
- 2 tbsp olive oil, plus more for greasing the dutch oven
- 4 cups of cooked rice
- salt and pepper, to taste

Instructions

1. Clean and grease your Dutch oven. Get your campfire going and prepare it so that there are enough hot coals for your Dutch oven to sit on.
2. Take the peppers' tops off. Take the pepper's central part apart and set the seeds aside. Cut the pepper tops off of the rest of the pepper. Cut it up and set it aside for stuffing.
3. In olive oil, cook the onion until it turns clear. Put in the chopped peppers, garlic, and mushrooms. It will take about 5 minutes of cooking until the vegetables are soft. Add the fake meat and stir it in. Cook for a few more minutes. Add the rice and about half of the tomato sauce can. Add pepper and salt.
4. After putting the peppers in the Dutch oven, stuff them with the stuffing. You can put some extra stuff around the peppers if you have some extra stuffing. Just make sure your Dutch oven is well-greased.
5. Add the ketchup to the rest of the tomato sauce and mix it in. Put some of the tomato sauce mix on top of the peppers that have been stuffed. Put some cheese on top of the peppers.
6. Make sure the Dutch oven is stable and level before putting hot coals on it. You might need to move some of the coals around to get it right or put a rock under the Dutch oven. Ensure the peppers are soft, and the stuffing is hot all through.

47. ENCHILADAS

Prep Time: 5 Minutes | Cook Time: 20 Minutes

Total Time: 25 Minutes | Serving: 4

Ingredients

- 1 tbsp cumin
- 2 cups of cheese
- 1 red bell pepper, cut into strips
- 2 tbsp oil
- 2 tsp salt
- 4-6 flour tortillas
- 14 ounce can enchilada sauce
- 1 cup of cooked black beans
- 4 cloves garlic, minced
- ½ red onion, sliced into thin half-moons

Instructions

1. So you can cook with embers, get your coals ready, or ignite your campfire.
2. Using medium-low heat, warm up the oil in a Dutch oven. Put in the peppers and cook them for a few minutes until they start to get soft. Add the onions and cook them with peppers until they are soft and clear. Add the salt, cumin, and garlic. Saute for 30 seconds, until the garlic smells good. Take the veggies off the heat and put them on a plate or bowl.
3. Ensure the Dutch oven's bottom is covered with 1/2 cup of enchilada sauce.
4. Set up the enchiladas by lining up the peppers and onions in the middle of a flour tortilla. Place some black beans on top and sprinkle cheese on top of that. Cover the fillings with the tortilla and roll it up. Place the enchilada in the Dutch oven seam side down. Do the same thing with the rest of the ingredients. How many enchiladas this recipe makes will depend on how big your Dutch oven is.
5. Put the rest of the sauce and cheese on top of the enchiladas. Put the lid on top of it.
6. You should put the Dutch oven back on the campfire. For indirect heat, the grill grate over the campfire works great. Then, put 14 to 16 coals on top of the lid. It should be cooked for 10 minutes or until the cheese melts.
7. Decorate with cilantro, jalapenos, and a squeeze of lime. Enjoy!

48. GUMBO

Prep Time: 30 Minutes | Cook Time: 4 Hour | Total Time: 4 Hour 30 Minutes | Serving: 10

Ingredients

- 4 slices bacon chopped in small pieces
- 1 (4 ounce) can green chilies
- 1 large green bell pepper chopped
- 1 pound andouille sausage sliced
- 3 pounds chicken thighs with bones
- 1 tsp dried basil
- 8 cups of chicken stock or 2
- 1/3 cup of vegetable oil
- 1/2 cup of all purpose flour
- 2 large onions chopped
- 1 (28 ounce) can diced tomatoes undrained
- 12 servings white rice cooked according to package directions
- 1 tsp dried thyme
- 1/2 tsp cayenne pepper
- 4 garlic cloves chopped
- 1/2 tsp black pepper
- 3 stalks celery chopped
- 1 pounds medium shrimp peeled and deveined
- 2 tsp salt
- Fresh parsley chopped (optional)

Instructions

1. Fire up a campfire and heat up a deep 12-inch Dutch oven. Cook bacon.
2. Put in the garlic, green chilies, onions, bell pepper, diced tomatoes, green chilies, chicken, sausage, thyme, basil, cayenne pepper, salt, and black pepper.
3. Cover and bring to a boil.
4. Cover and let it cook slowly for two hours. Note: for the gumbo to keep simmering slowly, you may need to lower the heat of the campfire at first and then add more firewood to keep the fire at the same level of heat. All of this depends on your elevation and the weather, so keep an eye on the gumbo and make any necessary changes to your campfire.
5. Take the chicken out of the Dutch oven and let it cool a bit. Then, take the meat off the bones and put the chicken back in the Dutch oven.
6. Put together the roux. Using a wire whisk, mix the oil and flour in a hot cast iron skillet until the roux starts to bubble. This will take about 5 minutes. Lower the heat by removing some campfire coals to keep the heat at a medium level. If you don't lower the heat while cooking, the roux will burn. Keep stirring the mixture until it starts to turn brown, and as it does, keep lowering the heat. Getting the roux to the deep color you want can take anywhere from 30 to 60 minutes.
7. When the roux turns brown, add the chicken stock slowly while stirring all the time.
8. It will start to boil after the chicken stock is added to the roux. After that, add it to the gumbo in the Dutch oven and stir it all together until it starts to simmer. When handling hot cooking tools, make sure you wear gloves that can withstand heat.
9. Put the shrimp right before serving and cook until they are no longer see-through.
10. Put in a bowl, pour over rice, and top with fresh parsley.

49. DUTCH OVEN CHILI

Prep Time: 15 Minutes | Cook Time: 1 Hour 15 Minutes

Total Time: 1 Hour 30 Minutes | Serving: 8

Ingredients

- 2 tbsp tomato paste
- 1 tsp garlic powder
- 7 ounces green chilies
- 1 cup of beef broth
- 1 large red bell pepper diced
- 30 ounces red kidney beans rinsed
- 1 small white onion diced
- 1/2 cup of finely crushed tortilla chips
- 1 tsp black pepper
- 2 tsp ground cumin
- 1 tsp salt
- 2 pounds beef chuck roast cut into 1 inch cubes
- 1 tbsp chili powder
- 3 ribs celery sliced
- 2 tsp paprika
- 2 tbsp vegetable oil
- 15 ounces diced tomatoes
- 1/4 cup of freshly chopped cilantro
- 1 cup of shredded cheddar cheese
- 1/2 cup of sour cream

Instructions

1. For about 5 minutes, heat a 12-inch (6-quart) cast iron Dutch oven by putting it on top of 15 briquettes. Add salt and pepper to the beef. Once the Dutch oven is hot, add the oil and brown the beef on all sides. Place the onion, red bell pepper, celery, and tomato paste in the pan. Saute for 5 to 7 minutes, until the vegetables get soft.
2. Let the spices cook for 60 to 90 seconds after adding the garlic powder, cumin, chili powder, and cumin.
3. Beans, diced tomatoes, green chilies, and beef broth should all be stirred in. Leave it to cook for an hour with the lid on.
4. Take off the lid and add the crushed tortilla chips. Let it sit uncovered for 10 minutes to get thicker. Cheese crumbles and chopped fresh cilantro can be added to it, or you can serve it plain.

50. CHICKEN AND VEGETABLES

Prep Time: 30 Minutes | Cook Time: 50 Minutes | Total Time: 1 Hour 20 Minutes | Serving: 6

Ingredients

- chicken thighs, boneless & skinless
- pepper
- water
- mushrooms
- salt
- carrot
- seasoning salt
- onion flakes
- sweet potato
- garlic powder

Instructions

1. Bricks of charcoal should be made for the Dutch oven.
2. Cut the vegetable into chunks after peeling it.
3. Stack the vegetables in the Dutch oven. First, we put down the carrots, then the sweet potatoes. On top of the vegetables, mix the onion flake, garlic powder, salt, and pepper.
4. On top, put the mushrooms. Put in a quarter cup of water. On top, put the chicken thighs. Put a lot of pepper, garlic powder, and seasoning salt on top.
5. Cover the Dutch oven with the lid.
6. Put at least 6 to 8 hot coals under the pot and 10 to 12 coals on top of the Dutch oven's lid. 50 to 60 minutes in the oven. Before you serve the chicken, make sure it's done.

51. ONE POT CHILI MAC

Prep Time: 5 Minutes | Cook Time: 15 Minutes | Total Time: 20 Minutes | Serving: 4

Ingredients

- ½ pound ground beef
- 8 ounce elbow noodles
- ½ cup of shredded cheddar cheese
- 1 tbsp cumin
- 2 tbsp chili powder
- 1 tbsp oil
- 1 tsp smoked paprika
- 1 ½ cup of broth, beef or vegetable
- 2 cloves garlic, minced
- 1 onion, diced
- 2 tbsp tomato paste
- 1 tsp sea salt
- 1 (14.5 ounce) can kidney beans

Instructions

- The oil should be heated over medium-low heat in a Dutch oven or another big pot with a lid. Three to five minutes later, add the onion and cook it until it turns clear.
- Season with salt, cumin, chili powder, smoked paprika, and tomato paste. Mix the tomato paste and spices into the meat by breaking it up with a spoon or spatula. Include the garlic after the meat has turned brown and cook for 30 to 60 seconds.
- While stirring, add the noodles, kidney beans, and broth. Replace the lid and cook for 5 to 6 minutes, unless the package of noodles says a different time.
- Take off the lid and add the cheese without mixing it in. Include your favorite chili toppings.

52. LASAGNA

Prep Time: 15 Minutes | Cook Time: 30 Minutes

Total Time: 45 Minutes | Serving: 6

Ingredients

- ➢ 2 tbsp Italian seasoning
- ➢ 2 cups of shredded mozzarella (fresh preferred), divided
- ➢ 15 ounce full-fat ricotta cheese
- ➢ 1 package no-boil lasagna noodles
- ➢ 28 ounce jar pasta sauce
- ➢ 1 tsp salt
- ➢ 15 ounce can spinach, drained (reserve liquid)

Instructions

1. Prepare Coals: Fire up the campfire and get the coals very hot. When the coals are hot, set about 15 of them aside so they are easy to get to. You will put them on top of your Dutch oven.
2. While that is going on, combine the ricotta, 1 ½ cups of mozzarella, spinach, salt, and herb mix. If you think it needs more seasoning, give it a taste.
3. Sprinkle ⅓ of the cheese mix on the Dutch oven's base and spread it out to cover it.
4. Put ⅓ of the pasta sauce on top of the cheese.
5. Place a layer of lasagna noodles on top. If the noodles are too big for the round pot, break them up. Do it again with the rest of the noodles, pasta sauce, and spinach cheese mixture (you may have some noodles left over).
6. Put the liquid you saved from the can of spinach into a measuring cup. Then, add water until you have ¾ cup of liquid. Along the edge of the lasagna, pour liquid. Put the rest of the mozzarella cheese on top of the mixture.
7. Cover the Dutch oven with the lid. There must be a flat lid on your Dutch oven if it's not a campfire-style oven. The lid must be turned upside down to hold the coals.
8. Put the Dutch oven right on top of the main pile of coals. Put the lid on top of the coals you saved with tongs, and bake for about 25 minutes.
9. Next, take off the lid and leave the Dutch oven on the fire for another five minutes without the lid on. The extra liquid needs to be boiled off. If it needs more time, cook it for a few more minutes until the extra liquid has dried out.
10. Take the Dutch oven off the heat. Let the lasagna cool down a bit before you serve it.

53. PIZZA

Prep Time: 20 Minutes | Cook Time: 20 Minutes

Total Time: 40 Minutes | Serving: 8

Ingredients

- ➢ 1 tbsp each flour + cornmeal
- ➢ 8-10 ounce pizza dough
- ➢ Toppings of choice

Instructions

1. PREPARE YOUR COALS: Get your coals or charcoal briquettes ready first. You need these numbers: 30 for a 10" Dutch oven and 33 for a 12" Dutch oven. Ensure the coals or briquettes are hot before putting the Dutch oven on the stove. Put 10 coals under the oven and 20 on top of the lid for a 10" oven. Put 11 coals under the oven and 22 on top of the lid for a 12" oven.
2. PREPARE THE DOUGH: Get your dough out and roll it out now. To make a circle with the dough, sprinkle flour on a cutting board and roll it out using a water bottle or wine bottle (because who brings a rolling pin camping?). Lightly sprinkle cornmeal on a piece of parchment paper. Then, move the dough to the paper. Indent the dough all over with a fork. This will keep it from rising while it's baking

TOP:

1. You can add any toppings you like.
2. Do the bake: Carefully take the Dutch oven off the heat and take off the lid. Cover the Dutch oven and go back to the bed of coals. Place the pizza in the oven with the parchment paper still on top. Place the spacers across the top and cover it. Put it in the oven for 15 to 20 minutes, or until the crust turns golden. SERVE AND ENJOY!

54. SPANISH STUFFED MINI PEPPERS

Prep Time: 10 Minutes | Cook Time: 20 Minutes

Total Time: 30 Minutes | Serving: 12

Ingredients

- 12 peppers
- 4 ounces Spanish chorizo
- 2 tsp flat leaf parsley
- 8 ounces goat cheese (chevre)

- 1 tsp fresh thyme leaves
- 2 shallots – minced
- ¼ cup of Spanish olives -(optional)
- fresh ground pepper

Vinaigrette:

- ¼ cup of sherry vinegar
- ¼ tsp sea salt
- ½ tsp fresh thyme leaves
- 1 tsp flat leaf parsley - minced

- 6 dates - pitted
- ⅔ cup of olive oil
- ½ tsp dijon mustard
- several grinds pepper

Garnishes:

- ¼ cup of slivered almonds - toasted

- fresh thyme and/or parsley

Instructions

1. If you use fresh peppers, cook them until they are soft. On high heat, bring them to a boil. Boil slowly for about one minute. Use cool water to rinse.
2. To use piquillo peppers, wash them and let them drain. Dry with a towel.
3. Warm the oven up to 375°.

The Goat Cheese Filling:

1. Over medium-high heat, cook the diced chorizo until the fat starts to render. Please put in the shallots and cook for about two minutes, until they get soft. A slotted spoon can be used to take the chorizo and shallot mix out of the fat and place it in a medium-sized prep bowl.
2. Melt the goat cheese and put it in a bowl. Add the chorizo, shallot, chopped olives, fresh herbs, sea salt, and a few grinds of pepper. Use a rubber spatula to mix everything together well.

Assemble the Mini Stuffed Peppers:

1. Now is the time to get your peppers ready, whether you're using fresh or piquillo.
2. Put the mixture into the peppers with a spoon. Fill the roasting pan with the items.
3. Please put them in an oven that has already been heated up. For piquillo peppers, it will take about 15 minutes, and for fresh peppers, it will take about 20 minutes.

The Date Vinaigrette:

1. Add the vinaigrette ingredients to the blender or food processor bowl simultaneously. With each pulse, make the mixture very smooth. Mix it better by adding some water if it's too thick.

To Serve:

1. Put some of the vinaigrette on top of each pepper. If you want, you can add toasted almonds and chopped fresh herbs as a garnish. Enjoy!

55. MAC & CHEESE

Prep Time: 5 Minutes | Cook Time: 10 Minutes

Total Time: 15 Minutes | Serving: 4

Ingredients

- 2 cups of elbow macaroni
- 1-2 tbsp mustard
- 5 ounce bag Kettle Brand Jalapeno chips
- 4 cups of cheddar cheese, shredded
- 2 tbsp butter
- 2 cups of water
- ¼ tsp garlic powder
- ¼ tsp salt

Instructions

1. Get your campfire or coals ready.
2. In a 4-quart Dutch oven, put the elbow macaroni, water, butter, and salt. Please cover it on top of a small bed of coals or embers. Add 10 to 15 coals to the top of the Dutch oven for about 10 minutes, or until the pasta is soft and most of the liquid is gone, but not all of it.
3. Take the Dutch oven off the fire and set the lid aside with care.
4. If you think it needs more salt, add it now, along with the shredded cheese, mustard, and garlic powder.
5. Please put it in bowls or on a plate, then sprinkle crushed Jalapeno Kettle Brand chips on top. Enjoy!

56. CAMPING TACOS

Prep Time: 20 Minutes | Cook Time: 1 Hour | Additional Time: 10

Total Time: 1 Hour 30 Minutes | Serving: 25

Ingredients

- 1 can diced tomatoes & green chilies
- 1 jar of salsa
- 1 package of corn tortillas (30-count)
- 1 28 ounce can enchilada sauce (red or green)
- 2 cans of beans, rinsed and drained
- 1 package Spanish rice mix
- 1 pound of ground meat
- 1 onion, diced
- 1 pound shredded cheddar cheese
- oil as needed
- optional: toppings of choice

Instructions

1. More than 35 charcoal briquettes should be made for the Dutch oven.
2. Use a little butter or oil to cook the onions until they become apparent.
3. When you add the meat, stir it around until it turns brown.
4. Put in the taco seasoning, tomato, and chili sauce liquid from the can. Let it cook for three to five minutes, adding water if necessary. Add the tomatoes, chilies, and beans and mix them in.
5. Find out how much water you need by reading the directions on the Spanish rice package. Add that much salsa instead of water along with the rest of the package. Do a thorough mix. Simmer for 5 minutes less than what it says on the package.
6. Put together a taco by putting ⅔ of the meat mixture into a tortilla.
7. Place the tacos in the Dutch oven so that they fit together tightly.
8. Add half of the enchilada sauce on top of the first round.
9. Add half of the cheese on top. Add another layer of tacos.
10. On top of the tacos, break up any leftover tortillas.
11. Put the rest of the sauce and cheese on top.
12. Cover the Dutch oven with a lid. 20 coals should go under the pot, and 15 should go on top of the lid. Place in the oven and add more coals for 60 to 75 minutes. Put on the toppings and eat!

57. SALISBURY STEAK

Prep Time: 20 Minutes | Cook Time: 1 Hour | Additional Time: 10 Minute

Total Time: 1 Hour 30 Minutes | Serving: 6

Ingredients

Patties:

- 1 egg
- 2 pounds ground beef
- 1 tsp minced garlic
- 1 tsp mustard
- 2 tsp Worchester sauce
- ½ cup of bread crumbs
- 1 tsp ketchup
- 1 tsp minced onion

Gravy:

- 1 package brown gravy mix
- 1 can cream of mushroom soup
- 1 can of water
- 1 package onion soup mix

Vegetables:

- 3 cups of new potatoes
- 2 cups of sliced mushrooms
- 2 cups of baby carrots

Instructions

1. Light more than 20 pieces of charcoal in a chimney.
2. Gather the patty's parts and mix them.
3. Mix the meat and spices together, then use your hands to make 6 big patties.
4. To make the gravy, mix the soup, water, gravy mix, and onion soup mix together. It is going to be bumpy! Put eight ready-to-use coals under the Dutch oven.
5. In the bottom of the Dutch oven, brown the patties on all sides. This was done in two sets of three. Put the carrots at the bottom of the Dutch oven.
6. Put the carrots on the bottom and the potatoes on top. Place the mushrooms on top of the potatoes. The steak patties should be put on top of the vegetables.
7. Cover the meat with the gravy. Cover the Dutch oven with the lid.
8. Put coals on top of the lid. There were about 12 coals on top and under the ovens, but we needed more heat because they were stacked on top of each other.
9. Put it in the oven for about an hour.

58. CAMPFIRE BRATWURST AND SAUERKRAUT

Prep Time: 5 Minutes | Cook Time: 20 Minutes

Total Time: 25 Minutes | Serving: 4

Ingredients

- 8 bratwurst or brat-style sausages
- 8 hot dog buns
- 1 cup of water
- 1 cup of stout beer I use Guinness
- 24 ounce jar sauerkraut
- brown spicy mustard

Instructions

1. Put the Dutch oven on a hot grate for the campfire. Put beer, sauerkraut, and water in the oven. Put the brats in the sauerkraut and cover the pot.
2. Cook brats that have already been cooked until they are warm through.
3. For brats that aren't already cooked, cook them until they reach the temperature listed on the package.
4. For a short time, the brats can stay in the sauerkraut until everyone is ready to eat. This meal can be eaten at a lot of different times. Also, the sausages should be taken out of the sauerkraut when the ends start to break.
5. Put a cast-iron frying pan on the campfire grate and wait for it to get hot. Move a few brats from the sauerkraut to the pan with tongs. Rotate the brats occasionally until they're charred all over, then take them off the heat.
6. It's okay to take the Dutch oven off the heat now if your campfire grate is too littel to fit both the Dutch oven and the skillet.
7. With the hot dog buns on the campfire grate and the sausages cooking in the pan, you can cook the sausages elsewhere. Let the buns toast, turning them every so often. Once the buns are toasted, take them off the heat and add the rest of the buns.
8. Put the brats and sauerkraut in the hot dog buns, and then add mustard on top.

59. MEATLOAF

Prep Time: 5 Minutes | Cook Time: 1 Hour | Total Time: 1 Hour 15 Minutes | Serving: 8

Ingredients

Meatloaf Ingredients:

- 1 pound ground beef
- 1 cup of Italian bread crumbs
- 1/2 tsp black pepper
- 3 cloves garlic minced
- 1 pound ground pork mild Italian sausage
- 4 slices regular cut bacon strips not thick cut
- 1 medium yellow onion chopped
- 2 tbsp Worcestershire sauce
- 3 large eggs beaten
- 1 8 ounce can tomato sauce
- 1 tsp salt

Glaze Ingredients:

- 1/4 cup of ketchup
- 1 tsp prepared mustard
- 2 tbsp packed brown sugar

Instructions

1. Special Equipment: Put parchment paper around the edges of your Dutch oven, or buy one already cut out.
2. Set your 12-inch Dutch oven to 350 degrees F for baking before you start.
3. Put the ketchup, brown sugar, and mustard in a small bowl and mix them. Set this bowl aside.
4. Add the ground beef, ground pork, mild Italian sausage, salt, black pepper, onion, and garlic to a large bowl. This is where you will mix the meatloaf ingredients. Then, add the bread crumbs. After that, the eggs were added. Then add the tomato sauce and Worcestershire sauce and mix well.
5. Use your hands to mix until everything is well blended. Refrain from mixing too much. Shape the meat mixture into a circle about 7 to 8 inches across.
6. Place bacon slices on top of the meatloaf in a pattern that looks like tic-tac-toe or a hashtag. It's like putting a lattice top on a pie.
7. Place the meatloaf mixture in the middle of the parchment paper. Use the paper corners sticking out as "handles" to lower the loaf into the oven that has already been heated.
8. Put the meatloaf in the middle of the oven and then pour the glaze mixture.
9. Put the meatloaf on the coals and cover it with the lid. Bake at 350°F degrees until it's done. Check the internal heat with a meat thermometer to ensure it reaches 165 degrees F. For even heating, turn the oven and lid 1/4 in opposite directions about every 15 minutes while the food is baking.
10. Take the Dutch oven off the coals and rest for 10 minutes. Then, use the handles made of parchment paper to lift it out, slice it, and serve.

60. OSSO BUCO WITH LEMON GREMOLATA

Prep Time: 20 Minutes | Cook Time: 3 Hour 30 Minutes

Total Time: 3 Hour 50 Minutes | Serving: 6

Ingredients

- ¾ cup of all-purpose flour
- 1 cup of beer
- 1 large onion, finely chopped
- 3 garlic cloves, finely chopped
- 1 ½ cup of kalamata olives, pitted & halved
- 2 tbsp unsated butter
- 1 tsp salt
- 1 bay leaf
- 2 tbsp extra virgin olive oil
- ¼ cup of chopped flat leaf parsley
- 1 garlic clove, diced
- 30 ounce canned diced tomatoes
- ½ tsp ground black pepper
- 1 large celery stalk, finely chopped
- 6 cross-cut veal shanks, approx. 1-pound each
- 3 sprigs of flat leaf parsley
- 2 tbsp + 2 tsp grated lemon zest
- 1 ½ tsp fresh thyme
- 1 cup of chicken broth
- 1 medium carrot, finely chopped

Instructions

1. Put salt and pepper to both sides of the shanks. Sprinkle flour on both sides of the shanks.
2. Put butter and olive oil in a large Dutch oven and heat it over high heat.
3. In two batches, brown the shanks on both sides for 10 to 12 minutes each. Set the shanks aside on a plate.
4. Turn the heat down to medium and put the onions, celery, carrots, and 3 chopped garlic cloves.
5. About 5 to 7 minutes of sauteing should get the vegetables soft and lightly browned.
6. Add the olives, thyme, bay leaf, 2 tbsp of lemon zest, beans, beer, and broth. Stir everything together. Before you add the shanks, bring the water to a boil.
7. Put the Dutch oven in the middle of the oven and cover the pot. Cook for about 2 ½ hours, or until the meat is very tender.
8. Mix ¼ cup of chopped parsley, 1 diced garlic clove, and 2 tsp of lemon zest together to make the gremolata. Throw away the bay leaf and parsley sprigs when the osso buco is done.
9. Add the gremolata on top and serve right away.

61. RED BEANS AND RICE

Prep Time: 15 Minutes | Cook Time: 1 Hour

Total Time: 1 Hour 15 Minutes | Serving: 6

Ingredients

- 1 small red bell pepper, diced
- 2 bay leaves
- ½ tsp dried thyme
- 6 cloves garlic minced
- ½ tbsp butter
- 1 large yellow onion, diced
- 1 tsp salt or to taste
- 14 ounces andouille sausage
- ½ cup of chopped fresh parsley plus more for garnish
- 1 tsp dried oregano
- 3 15 ounce cans red beans
- 2 celery ribs, diced
- 2 tbsp olive oil
- 1 small green bell pepper, diced
- 6 to 7 cups of low sodium vegetable broth
- ½ tsp paprika
- 1 ½ cups of long grain brown rice
- ⅛ tsp ground cayenne red pepper
- Freshly ground black pepper
- Fresh green onions chopped, plus more for garnish

Instructions

1. Heat the coals and the Dutch oven, then add the oil. Put the sausage slices in the oil that is already hot and cook them until both sides are browned. Add more often. The sausage should be taken out of the pot and set aside. Combine butter with the pot and melt it.
2. Over medium-low heat, put the onions and cook for three minutes, until they start to get soft.
3. Keep cooking for 4 minutes after adding the celery and bell peppers. If it needs it, add a little more butter. Include garlic and cook for 15 seconds.
4. Add black pepper, oregano, thyme, paprika, cayenne, and salt. Cook for one more minute. Add the vegetable broth and stir it in, making sure to get all the browned bits off the bottom of the pot. Include bay leaves. Bring the mix to a rolling boil.
5. Turn down the heat, cover, and wait 45 to 60 minutes.
6. Add one cup of cooked rice to the mix.
7. Take out one cup of beans and mash them with the back of a fork. Add the beans back to the pot and stir them around. You can add up to a cup of water if it's too thick.
8. Check the food for salt and seasonings and make any necessary changes.
9. Put the green onions and parsley, and cook for 5 more minutes.
10. Do not heat up anymore. Spread on top of rice that has been cooked.

62. CAMPFIRE TACO IN A BAG

Prep Time: 10 Minutes | Cook Time: 15 Minutes

Total Time: 25 Minutes | Serving: 4

Ingredients

- ➢ 1 cup of shredded lettuce
- ➢ 1 packet of taco seasoning
- ➢ 1 pound lean ground hamburger
- ➢ 3/4 cup of cherry tomatoes, quartered
- ➢ 1/2 cup of salsa
- ➢ 1 cup of shredded cheddar cheese
- ➢ 1/2 cup of sour cream
- ➢ 4-5 individual serving size taco chip bags

Instructions

1. Warm up the campfire so you can cook. Read the piece called How to Build a Cooking Fire.
2. Put the thawed hamburger in a medium-sized foil pan and set it over the fire. Once it starts cooking, use a metal spatula to break the meat into pieces. Keep doing this every couple of minutes until the meat is browned.
3. There shouldn't be any extra grease because the meat is cooking over a campfire, but if there is, pour it into a Styrofoam cup or a paper plate and throw it away.
4. Sprinkle the taco seasoning and 3/4 cup of water over the hamburger and put it back over the fire. Mix the meat until it is well-coated. For another 5 minutes, or until the seasoning has thickened and most of the water has evaporated, stir the food every now and then. Crush the taco chips in each of the four bags, and then cut off the top of one side of each bag with scissors.
5. Spread a lot of hamburger on top of the crushed taco chips. Add cheese, tomatoes, lettuce, salsa, or any other toppings you like. I make salsa that isn't too spicy for the kids, but you can add hot sauce or make it more spicy for other people. Simple to clean up!

63. FOIL PACK CAMPFIRE COOKED SALMON

Prep Time: 5 Minutes | Cook Time: 25 Minutes

Total Time: 30 Minutes | Serving: 4

Ingredients

- ➢ 1 Lemon
- ➢ 1 Medium Sized Piece Salmon with skin
- ➢ Pinch Salt
- ➢ Pinch Black Pepper

Instructions

1. Get the wood or coals for your campfire nice and hot.
2. Cut two pieces of foil in half and place them on top of each other.
3. Place your salmon piece on top of the aluminum foil. Sprinkle as much salt and pepper as you like on top of the salmon, and then put thin slices of lemon over the meaty part of the fish. Next, seal the aluminum foil all the way around so there are no holes or leaks.
4. You should put your foil package in the fire. It was put right on the hot "bed" or coal area.
5. To make sure the salmon is fully cooked, you will need a meat thermometer at this point.
6. Every eight minutes or so, turn your foil packet over in the fire. Because every campfire heats up differently, it's hard to say how long you can cook over the fire.
7. After cooking ours for about 25 minutes, we used a meat thermometer to make sure it was done.
8. We knew it was done when the meat thermometer read more than 145 degrees.

64. CAMPFIRE SHRIMP BOIL

Prep Time: 5 Minutes | Cook Time: 20 Minutes

Total Time: 25 Minutes | Serving: 2

Ingredients

- ½ tsp sea salt, divided
- 1 tsp Old Bay Seasoning
- 12 ounces baby potatoes (~10 potatoes)
- 1 pound mussels
- 12-ounce can beer
- 4 ounces shrimp, shells removed and deveined, tails on or off as desired
- 2 corn on the cob, shucked + halved
- 1 lemon, cut into thick slices
- ½ yellow or sweet onion, peeled + cut into wedges
- 2 tbsp butter or ghee, plus more for serving if desired
- Cocktail sauce (to serve)

Instructions

1. Prepare campfire: Get the coals very hot or let a campfire burn out until the wood is smoldering but there are no more flames.
2. Put parchment paper inside the Dutch oven so the food doesn't stick to the pot.
3. For the Dutch oven, add the potatoes, beer, onion, lemon, Old Bay, and salt.
4. The pot should be covered and put on the coals. It will take about 15 minutes of cooking to get the potatoes soft.
5. Take the oven off the heat and add the butter, corn, shrimp, and mussels.
6. Put the oven back on the coals and cover it. Cook for another 5 minutes (or 10 minutes if the seafood is frozen) or until the shrimp is opaque and the mussels are open.
7. Take the mixture off the heat and put it on plates or bowls. For every serving, add some of the broth from the oven.
8. Serve with lots of napkins, extra butter, and cocktail sauce.

65. OREGON COAST CAMPFIRE PAELLA

Prep Time: 15 Minutes | Cook Time: 45 Minutes

Total Time: 1 Hour | Serving: 2

Ingredients

- ½ tsp paprika
- 1 medium onion, , minced
- 4 cloves garlic, , minced
- 1 pound seafood, (mussels, clams, shrimp, prawns, or a mix)
- Big pinch of saffron
- 1 cup of short grained rice, , Bomba is traditional if you can find it; we used Calrose

- 15 cherry tomatoes
- 1 ½ cup of broth
- ½ tsp red pepper flakes
- ½ cup of Kenwood Vineyards Sauvignon Blanc
- 3 tbsp olive oil
- 2 tsp salt
- Parsley, , to garnish

Instructions

1. Clean the mussels and clams, remove the beards from the mussels, and devein the shrimp or prawns if they still need to be done. In a large bowl, cover the mussels and clams with cold water. Let them soak while you prepare the other ingredients.

2. Start a campfire. You won't need to burn the wood down to embers because you'll be cooking over the flames. Put your cast iron on the grill to get it hot. Step you can skip: Poke holes in the cherry tomatoes and put them on the grill over the fire to roast. This gives the paella a nice smokey taste and brings out some of the sweetness in the tomatoes.

3. Put 1 and a half cups of broth into a cup of or small bowl. Stir the saffron into the broth after adding it. Put away. Cut the garlic and onion into small pieces.

4. When the pan is hot from the fire, put the olive oil, then the diced onion, salt, and red pepper flakes. For about two minutes, until the onion starts to get soft, saute.

5. Put the rice and garlic that has been chopped into the pan. Toast the rice for two to three minutes, stirring it often, until it starts to turn golden (but not brown). Stir in the wine and wait about three minutes for the rice to soak it up.

6. Stir the rice for a moment to coat it with the paprika. Then add the saffron-flavored broth and baked tomatoes. You can leave it alone after giving it a good stir to spread out the ingredients. It's time to add the mussels, clams, and shrimp! Add another 15 minutes of cooking time. The paella is done when the rice is soft, all the liquid has been absorbed, and you can hear the rice "crackling." This means that the socarrat, the deliciously crunchy brown crust that paella is known for, is forming.

7. Take it off the heat, add the parsley, and enjoy it with the rest of the wine!

66. SALMON COUSCOUS BAKE

Prep Time: 5 Minutes | Cook Time: 20 Minutes | Total Time: 25 Minutes | Serving: 4

Ingredients

- 1 lemon, sliced
- 8 ounces green beans
- 2 cups of broth
- 1 tsp Italian herb mix
- 10 ounce box plain couscous
- 1 cup of halved cherry tomatoes
- ¼ cup of capers (optional)
- 2 tbsp oil (or butter)
- ½ tsp sea salt, divided
- 4 salmon fillets

Instructions

1. Prepare campfire: Get the coals very hot or let a campfire burn out until the wood is smoking, but there are no more flames.
2. Place a piece of parchment paper inside the Dutch oven to keep the couscous from sticking to the pot. Add a little salt to the salmon fillets and set them aside.
3. Add the couscous, broth, capers, oil, Italian seasoning, and the rest of the salt in a Dutch oven. Mix it all together. On top of the couscous, add the green beans and tomatoes.
4. Place the salmon fillets inside the couscous and vegetables. Place the lemon slices on top of the fish.Place the oven on coals and cover it. After 20 minutes, the salmon should be easy to flake apart with a fork. Take it off the heat and serve right away.

67. STEAMED CLAMS

Prep Time: 15 Minutes | Cook Time: 13 Minutes | Total Time: 28 Minutes | Serving: 2

Ingredients

- 2 cloves garlic, minced
- ½ tsp red pepper flakes
- fresh parsley
- 1 lemon, cut into quarters
- Crusty baguette, sliced
- ¾ cup of white wine
- 2 pounds littleneck clams
- 2 tbsp butter

Instructions

1. Check the clams and throw away any that aren't closed. If any are open on the table, tap them; if they close within a few minutes, continue using them. The clams need to be cleaned.
2. Set the Dutch oven (or pot with a tight-fitting lid) over medium heat and melt the butter. Once the foaming stops, add the garlic and red pepper flakes and mix them in.
3. While there should still be liquid in the pot, add the wine and let it simmer for about 30 seconds, just until the alcohol burns off.
4. Incorporate the clams and cover the pot with a lid. After 5 to 10 minutes of steaming, the clams should be open. Remove any clams that are still closed and throw them away.
5. Garnish with lemon juice, parsley, and grilled bread to soak up all the sauce!

68. CAMPING DUTCH OVEN STEAK

Prep Time: 5 Minutes | Cook Time: 30 Minutes | Marinating Time: 12 Hours

Total Time: 12 Hours 35 Minutes | Serving: 4

Ingredients

Marinade Ingredients:

- ➢ 1 tbsp Sriracha hot sauce
- ➢ 1 tbsp Worcestershire sauce
- ➢ 1/3 cup of soy sauce
- ➢ 1 tbsp olive oil

Steak & Potatoes Ingredients:

- ➢ 2 tbsp olive oil
- ➢ 1/2 tsp dried thyme
- ➢ 4 garlic cloves minced
- ➢ 1/2 tsp dried rosemary
- ➢ 4 tbsp unsalted butter
- ➢ Fresh parsley optional
- ➢ 1.5 pound flank steak fat trimmed and sliced against the grain into thin strips
- ➢ 1/4 tsp crushed red pepper flakes
- ➢ 1.5 pounds petite fingerling potatoes quartered

Instructions

1. Put the soy sauce, Worcestershire sauce, olive oil, and Sriracha in a gallon-sized plastic bag that can be closed. Put the steak strips in the bag, close it, and toss the meat to coat it. Put it in the fridge or cooler for 12 to 24 hours to marinate.
2. Put the olive oil and potato wedges in a 12-inch Dutch oven that is on medium-high heat. It will take about 15 to 20 minutes of stirring every now and then until the potato wedges are golden and soft. Take the potatoes out, set them aside, and cover them to keep them warm.
3. Put the butter in the Dutch oven and let it melt. Then add the pepper flakes, garlic, thyme, and rosemary, and stir constantly until the garlic smells good. It will only take a minute, so be careful not to burn it.
4. Scrub the steak strips clean before adding them to the pot. For about 5 minutes, stir them as they cook until they turn brown. The steak strips should only be lightly browned on all sides. Do not cook them for too long.
5. To finish cooking, put the lid back on the pot and add the potato wedges back in. Stir them in with the other ingredients. Cook for another two minutes.
6. Take the Dutch oven off the heat, sprinkle parsley on top, and serve hot.

69. COUNTRY-STYLE PORK RIBS

Prep Time: 15 Minutes | Cook Time: 2 Hour 15 Minutes | Total Time: 2 Hour 30 Minutes | Serving: 4

Ingredients

- 1 tsp cumin
- 1 tbsp oregano
- 1 tbsp garlic salt
- 1 tsp black pepper
- 1 tbsp parsley
- 1 tsp smoked paprika
- 2 pounds country-style ribs
- 3 tbsp olive oil
- bbq sauce

Instructions

1. Make a dry rub with black pepper, oregano, parsley, cumin, garlic salt, and oregano.
2. Use the dry rub you made to coat all sides of the country-style ribs.
3. Put the Dutch oven on the stove over medium heat and add the olive oil. Once the oil is shiny, add the ribs to the pot. Try to sear them well on all sides.
4. Get the oven hot, about 350°F. If you put the lid on top of the Dutch oven, put it in the oven for 1,5 hours.Take the pot out of the oven, uncover the ribs, and coat them with a lot of BBQ sauce. Bring the oven down to 325 degrees F. Put the ribs back in the oven, but this time leave the door open for another 30 minutes.
5. Take the ribs out of the pot and put them on a platter. They may fall apart, or you can use a fork to cut them up into smaller pieces. Cover them with more BBQ sauce with a brush before you serve them. Enjoy.

70. CARNITAS

Prep Time: 30 Minutes | Cook Time: 1 Hour | Total Time: 2 Hours 10 Minutes | Serving: 4

Ingredients

- 3-5 pound boneless pork butt
- 2-3 tbsp of Mexican carnitas spice
- 2 onions
- 1 can of beer
- 2 oranges
- 2 lemons
- 1 pound of bacon
- 1 jar salsa

Instructions

1. Set up the charcoal briquettes for a bake at 325°F. Temperature Chart for a Dutch Oven
2. Season the pork roast with the carnitas mix. Cut the onion and bacon, and cook them in the Dutch oven's bottom. Use the bacon grease to brown the pork on all sides.
3. Put the pork in the pot. Put the salsa and beer on top of the meat.
4. Cut up the oranges and lemons or limes and put them in the pot.
5. Put a lid on it and cook for 20 minutes for every pound. If you need to, add time. When the pork is easy to shred, it's done. Take the pork off the heat, shred it, drain the liquid, and put it back in the hot oven for a few minutes to crisp up.

71. BEEF STROGANOFF

Prep Time: 15 Minutes | Cook Time: 45 Minutes

Total Time: 60 Minutes | Serving: 6

Ingredients

- 1 1/2 pound flat iron steak cut into thin strips against the grain
- 1 pound mostaccioli (or extra wide egg noodles)
- 1/4 tsp black pepper
- 2 tbsp soy sauce
- 1 (32 ounce) carton beef broth + water if necessary
- 1 bunch fresh parsley chopped (optional)
- 4 cloves garlic minced
- 1 (8 ounce) package fresh sliced mushrooms (white or cremini mushrooms)
- 2 tbsp vegetable oil
- 1 tsp salt
- 1 medium onion diced
- 1 cup of sour cream
- 2 tbsp Dijon mustard

Instructions

1. Get your camp stove or fire ready to cook.
2. Get the vegetables ready and cut up the meat.
3. Use a medium-high heat campfire or stove to warm up a 12-inch cast iron Dutch oven.
4. Put the oil in the pot.
5. Pour the steak into the Dutch oven and stir it to sear all sides—season with salt and pepper. Take the meat out of the pot and cover it to keep it warm.
6. Turn the heat to medium and saute the onion and mushrooms for a while. Then add the garlic and cook until it softens.
7. Put the beef broth, mustard, and soy sauce in the Dutch oven. Turn up the heat to high, cover, and stir it now and then while it cooks until it boils.
8. Place the pasta in the water when it starts to boil. Stir it a few times until it's done how you like it. This food needs more time to cook than what the package says.
9. Stir the meat back into the Dutch oven to mix it with the other things.
10. Slowly warm the sour cream by adding small amounts of the hot mixture while stirring it. This will keep it from curdling when you add it to the Dutch oven.
11. Add the sour cream slowly while taking the Dutch oven off the heat. Stir it in until it's thoroughly mixed in. If you want, sprinkle parsley on top and serve.

72. PULLED PORK

Prep Time: 15 Minutes | Cook Time: 5 Hour

Total Time: 5 Hour 15 Minutes | Serving: 10

Ingredients

- 3 Onions
- 2 tbsp Salt
- 2 tins Tomatoes
- 1 tsp Freshly Ground Pepper
- 4,5 pound Neck of Pork
- 1 cup of Chicken Stock
- 2 tbsp Smoked Paprika
- 1 pound Smoky Barbecue Sauce
- 1 Garlic
- Water
- Olive oil

Instructions

1. Start a fire or 20 charcoal briquettes.
2. TIP: The charcoal will help you keep the heat just right while you cook. About 12 pieces of charcoal should go on the bottom and 8 should go on top. The temperature should be around 260°F (125°C). Get the meat dry.
3. The dry ingredients should all be mixed together.The dry spices should be rubbed into the meat. Peel and cut the onions and garlic into small pieces.
4. Place a few tbsp of oil in the bottom of your Dutch oven. (I use a little more than I would in a regular oven because it burns off quickly over the fire.)
5. Put the meat in the Dutch oven.
6. TIP: Put the fattier side of the meat in the Dutch oven if there is more fat on one side than the other. This will help your meat not burn and stick together.
7. Put the garlic and onions in there. Put in the canned tomatoes, stock, and any barbecue sauce you like.
8. They will also work if you use tomatoes from your garden; just cut them up pretty small and add them to the pot. Based on the size of your tomatoes, you will need 4 to 6 of them to replace a tin.
9. Include enough water to cover the meat. Check on it every 5 hours to make sure it doesn't dry out. It's done when the meat falls apart when you pull on it with a fork. It will take six hours.

73. DUTCH OVEN POT ROAST

Prep Time: 10 Minutes | Cook Time: 4 Hour

Total Time: 4 Hour 10 Minutes | Serving: 10

Ingredients

- ➤ Roast 2.5–3 pounds
- ➤ Carrots - 1.5 carrots per person. Peeled and cut into 3″ slices.
- ➤ Salt and Pepper to taste
- ➤ Onion(s) One Large. Sliced into quarters and separated.
- ➤ Beef broth, beef stock, or beef bullion. If using beef broth or beef stock, use in place of water. If using beef bullion use one tsp of paste or two cubes.
- ➤ Cream of Mushroom Soup (1.5 cups or one can condensed)
- ➤ Water 8 ounce
- ➤ Potatoes - 1.5 per person. Peeled and cut into quarters.
- ➤ 4 cloves of Garlic, crushed
- ➤ 4 Tbsp Worcestershire Sauce
- ➤ 2 bay leaves (optional)

Instructions

1. Warm the oven up to 325F. Put the roast in the Dutch oven.
2. Add 1 tbsp of Worcestershire sauce, salt, and pepper to each side of your roast.
3. Put in your onions. You can add the vegetables to the roast at the start of cooking or after an hour. Since I like mine soft, I put them in at the start. If adding at the start, salt and pepper the vegetables and pour the rest of the Worcestershire sauce over them.
4. Bullion paste, cubes, water, broth, or stock should be added.
5. Put your mushroom cream soup on top of everything.
6. Put the Dutch oven in the oven with the lid on.
7. After three hours, check to see if it's done. If you twist the roast with a fork, it should fall apart. If it's hard to twist the fork, cook for another hour and try again.
8. Take the roast out of the oven and let it rest for ten minutes.
9. Use the pot liquor in the bottom of the Dutch oven for gravy. You can also clean out the pan and make your own gravy.

74. PORK CHOPS AND RICE

Prep Time: 5 Minutes | Cook Time: 35 Minutes

Total Time: 40 Minutes | Serving: 4

Ingredients

- ➢ 3 medium tomatoes quartered
- ➢ 1 14 ounce can beef broth
- ➢ 4 bone-in pork chops medium thickness
- ➢ 1 green bell pepper thinly sliced
- ➢ 2 cloves garlic minced
- ➢ 1 cup of uncooked jasmine rice
- ➢ 1 medium onion chopped
- ➢ 1/2 tsp oregano
- ➢ Salt and pepper to taste
- ➢ 2 tbsp Worcestershire sauce
- ➢ 2 tbsp olive oil
- ➢ Fresh parsley chopped (optional)

Instructions

1. A campfire, camp stove, or charcoal briquettes can be used to heat a 12-inch cast iron Dutch oven over medium heat.
2. Put oil in a pot and heat it up. Season the pork chops with pepper and salt , then add them to the Dutch oven and brown them on both sides. If you have to, work in groups.
3. Take the chops out of the oven.
4. In the oven's bottom, mix the rice, Worcestershire sauce, and beef broth together.
5. The pork chops should be put back in the pot on top of the rice.
6. Place chops on a baking sheet. Add bell pepper, onion, garlic, and tomatoes. Then, sprinkle oregano on top of everything.
7. Cover and cook on medium-low heat for about 20-30 minutes, or until the pork chops are done and the rice is soft.
8. Add fresh parsley on top to serve.

75. BEEF STEW

Prep Time: 10 Minutes | Cook Time: 1 Hour

Total Time: 1 Hour 10 Minutes | Serving: 1

Ingredients

- 3 cups of beef broth
- 1 medium yellow onion, diced
- 5 Red Potatoes (chopped)
- 1 pound beef, cubed
- 1/2 tsp thyme
- Can of baked beans
- 2 tbsp Worcestershire sauce
- 1 Potato (peeled and chopped)
- 2 garlic cloves, minced
- salt & pepper

Instructions

1. Remove any fat from the beef and cut it into small cubes.
2. Put the beef, onion, and garlic in a big cast iron pot.
3. Put the meat on medium heat and brown it.
4. Add all the vegetables and the rest of the items to the pot and mix them together.
5. Let it cook for 45 minutes before serving.

76. PORK CHOPS

Prep Time: 15 Minutes | Cook Time: 40 Minutes

Total Time: 55 Minutes | Serving: 6

Ingredients

- 6 cloves Garlic (peeled, smashed)
- 1 Medium onion (sliced thin)
- 1/4 cup of Fresh parsley (chopped)
- Salt and pepper to taste
- 1 cup of Chicken broth
- 1 tsp Dried thyme leaves
- 4 tbsps Vegetable oil
- 1 tbsp Brown sugar
- 1 pkg Fresh mushrooms (8-ounce package, sliced)
- 6 Meyer Heritage Duroc Bone-In Center Cut Pork Chops
- 1 cup of Cider vinegar

Instructions

1. Start a campfire or some other way to cook.
2. Warm up the oil in the bottom of a 12-inch camp Dutch oven.
3. Put salt and pepper to both sides of the pork chops.
4. In the Dutch oven, brown the pork chops on both sides with the hot oil.
5. Now put the butter, garlic, mushrooms, onion, brown sugar, thyme, and chicken broth into the camp Dutch oven. Cover and cook for about 40 minutes, or until the chops are soft. Add parsley on top to serve.

77. DUTCH OVEN CHICKEN

Prep Time: 10 Minutes | Cook Time: 45 Minutes | Total Time: 55 Minutes | Serving: 4

Ingredients

- 1 head garlic
- 1 1/2 tsp black pepper
- 1/2 tsp onion powder
- 3 1/2 tsp kosher salt
- Baby potatoes, carrots, and an onion
- 2 tsp chopped fresh thyme
- Whole chicken
- Butter
- 1 tsp paprika

Instructions

1. Put pepper, salt, paprika, onion powder, and thyme on the chicken and rub it all over.
2. Set the Dutch oven over hot coals and melt the butter with the garlic cloves. Then sear the chicken with the breast side down.
3. Take out the chicken and add the vegetables. Then, place the chicken on top of the vegetables with the breast side facing up.Put the meat thermometer into the part that is the thickest.
4. Place hot coals on top of the lid and cook until the temperature is right. 165 degrees.

78. CREAMY CAJUN CHICKEN CAMPING PASTA

Prep Time: 5 Minutes | Cook Time: 25 Minutes | Total Time: 30 Minutes | Serving: 4

Ingredients

- 1 can fire roasted tomatoes
- 1 small jalapeno pepper diced
- 2 containers chicken broth
- 1 (8 ounce) package cream cheese
- 1 tbsp Cajun seasoning
- 1 (16 ounce) package farfalle pasta
- 2 pre-cooked chicken breasts
- Salt and pepper to taste
- Fresh parsley optional

Instructions

1. Use a campfire, camp stove, or RV stove to cook the chicken broth over high heat in a 12-inch cast iron Dutch oven.
2. Cover the pot and cook the pasta for about 5 to 10 minutes, or until it is al dente but still firm to the bite. Don't pour any water out of the pot.
3. Lower the heat to medium-high and put the tomatoes, cream cheese, Jalapeno, salt, and pepper. Stir in the chicken.
4. Cover and cook until the chicken is hot and the cream cheese melts, stirring every now and then. After taking off the lid, keep cooking until the sauce is the thickness you want it to be, which should take about 5 to 10 minutes.
5. You can put fresh parsley on top if you want, and serve hot.

79. CHICKEN AND SQUASH CASSEROLE

Prep Time: 10 Minutes | Cook Time: 1 Hour

Total Time: 1 Hour 10 Minutes | Serving: 5

Ingredients

- 2 12.5 ounce Cans Chunk Chicken (or 2-3 boneless skinless chicken breasts chopped into small chunks)
- 1/2 Cup of Water (extra 3/4 cup needed if using fresh chicken and not canned)
- 1 Box Chicken Flavored Stuffing Mix
- 1 10.5 ounce Can Cream Of Mushroom Soup
- 2 Tbsp Oil (used avocado oil)
- 2 Fresh Yellow Squash
- 1 4 ounce Can Sliced Mushrooms
- No-Stick Cooking Spray
- 2 Fresh Zucchini

Instructions

1. Start the fire an hour to thirty minutes before you start cooking. If you want to cook over a fire, let it burn down a bit first. Then add hot coals.
2. Put oil, water, soup, mushrooms (with liquid from can), and both cans of chicken (with liquid from can) into a large bowl. Be sure to mix the ingredients well.
3. Peel and cut the squash and zucchini into small pieces.
4. Slice the squash and zucchini and add them to the soup.
5. Throw the dry stuffing mix into the bowl and mix it well.
6. Spray the inside of the Dutch oven with the nonstick spray. Put the casserole mix into the Dutch oven.
7. Put the Dutch oven next to the fire. It should be raised about 10 to 12 inches above the heat. Put the lid on.
8. Give it fifty minutes to cook. Every 20 minutes, switch sides so that the same side isn't facing the heat. It will be really hot, so be very careful when you move it.
9. When the cookies are done cooking for an hour, crack the lid in the last 10 minutes to let some steam escape and dry them out a bit.

80. CHICKEN WITH PASTA & CHEESE

Prep Time: 15 Minutes | Cook Time: 20 Minutes | Additional Time: 10

Total Time: 45 Minutes | Serving: 8

Ingredients

- ➢ 1 pound boneless skinless chicken breasts
- ➢ 1-2 cups of shredded cheese
- ➢ 12 ounce pasta, rigatoni or your favorite
- ➢ 4 cloves garlic, minced
- ➢ 1 onion
- ➢ 2 tbsp olive oil
- ➢ 2 tbsp cup of butter
- ➢ 12 ounce pasta sauce
- ➢ salt & pepper to taste

Instructions

1. To partly cook the pasta, boil it for half the suggested time. Put it aside after rinsing it with cold water.
2. Warm up the Dutch oven over campfire coals or 10 to 12 ready-made charcoal briquettes.
3. Make big pieces of the chicken.
4. In the cast iron pot, start cooking the chicken with butter and olive oil. Stir the chicken often as it cooks. After a while, add the onion and cook it.
5. After you add the garlic, cook for one or two more minutes.
6. Add the pasta sauce when the chicken is almost done cooking. Stir it in and let it cook for a few minutes. Put in some salt and pepper.
7. Add the cheese and half-cooked pasta and mix them together. Take the pot off the fire.
8. Place the coals or briquettes on top of the pot's lid. Let it cook for 10 minutes. Serve and Enjoy.

81. LEMON CHICKEN

Prep Time: 5 Minutes | Cook Time: 50 Minutes

Total Time: 55 Minutes | Serving: 4

Ingredients

- ➤ 4 large sprigs fresh rosemary torn into smaller pieces
- ➤ 2 tbsp olive oil
- ➤ 1 lemon divided using 1/2 thinly sliced, 1/2 juiced (If you want a really robust lemon flavor, use two lemons)
- ➤ Water or chicken broth if necessary
- ➤ 8 cloves garlic peeled and left whole
- ➤ Salt and black pepper to taste
- ➤ 12 petite potatoes sliced in half
- ➤ 8 bone-in skin-on chicken thighs rinse, then pat chicken dry with paper towel
- ➤ 1 medium onion sliced

Instructions

1. Follow the directions to get your ingredients, heat source, and tools ready.
2. Use 29 campfire coals or charcoal briquettes to heat up a 12-inch cast iron Dutch oven to 400 degrees F and roast chicken. Keep in mind that you might need two sets of coals to finish cooking, so be ready to start the second set when the first set is about half-way done. Put salt and pepper on all sides of the chicken.
3. To make a medium-high heat for browning the chicken, put all the coals below the Dutch oven. Fill the pot with olive oil before you start cooking.
4. Put the chicken in the pan skin side down and sear it. Then flip it over and brown all sides. After 10 minutes, the chicken should be a nice golden brown color. Take it out and set it aside.
5. Get the brown bits off the bottom of the pan and add the lemon juice.
6. Put the potatoes, onions, and garlic in the Dutch oven and stir them all together.
7. Place lemon slices and rosemary sprigs inside the dish on top of the potatoes. Then, put the chicken on top, skin side up. (You want the skin to stay crispy.)
8. At 400°F degrees, move 19 coals to the top of the lid and leave 10 coals below the oven. Cover with the lid and bake for 30 to 40 minutes, or until the chicken is cooked through and the potatoes are soft. Every 15 minutes or so, turn the oven and lid 1/4 turn in the opposite direction to make sure the baking is even. NOTE: If the potatoes aren't soft but all the water has been absorbed, add a little water (or chicken broth if you have it) and keep cooking until the potatoes are soft. The 165°F temperature on a meat thermometer should show that the thigh is fully cooked.
9. Put vegetables on a plate, then chicken on top of them, and pour sauce over everything. Warm up and serve.

82. SPRITE CHICKEN

Prep Time: 30 Minutes | Cook Time: 1 Hour

Total Time: 1 Hour 30 Minutes | Serving: 6

Ingredients

- ➤ 1/2 pound bacon cut in bite-size pieces
- ➤ 1 pound baby carrots
- ➤ 2 pounds russet potatoes peeled, rinsed, and cut in 1-inch cubes
- ➤ 14 inch Dutch Oven
- ➤ 1/4 cup of all-purpose flour
- ➤ 6 ounces Sprite (lemon-lime soda)
- ➤ 1 yellow onion chopped
- ➤ 2 pounds boneless, skinless chicken breasts cut in 1-inch cubes
- ➤ 1/2 Tbsp seasoned salt

Instructions

1. Fry bacon until it's crispy in a Dutch oven on a camp chef or on the stove. With a slotted spoon, take out the bacon pieces, leaving the grease inside. Leave the bacon alone.
2. In a large gallon plastic bag, mix together the seasoned salt and flour. To coat the chicken, add it to the flour mixture and shake it around. Brown the chicken pieces in bacon grease after adding them to the Dutch oven.
3. Take the chicken out and set it aside.
4. Put the potatoes, carrots, chicken, bacon, and onions in the Dutch oven in this order. Add Sprite all over the top. Put the lid on top.
5. Put it in the oven at 350° F for one hour. Take it out of the oven carefully. Take the lid off and let it sit for 5 minutes before serving.
6. Campsite cooking:
7. Do what it says above. Put the Dutch oven in hot coals and cover it with a lid when you cook. It should be cooked for 45 minutes to an hour, or until the chicken is done and the vegetables are soft.

83. CHICKEN MARBELLA

Prep Time: 5 Minutes | Cook Time: 45 Minutes

Total Time: 50 Minutes | Serving: 4-6

Ingredients

- 2 tbsp dried oregano
- ¼ cup of capers
- ½ cup of dry white wine
- 1 cup of Mediterranean or Greek olives, pitted & halved
- 6 cloves garlic, roughly chopped
- 1 cup of chopped prunes
- 2 bay leaves
- 4 chicken thighs, skin on
- 1 tbsp olive oil
- 1 tsp salt
- ¼ cup of red wine vinegar
- 4 tsp brown sugar

Instructions

1. Put chicken in the marinade for 6 to 24 hours. This isn't necessary, but it does help all of these great flavors blend into the chicken. Put everything together except the oil and brown sugar, and keep it cool in the fridge or ice chest.
2. Set up the fire. You'll need about twenty charcoal briquettes or coals from the campfire. A hot Dutch oven, about 425 degrees, is what you need. When the coals are hot, flatten them out and put the Dutch oven on top.
3. Brown chicken: Put 1 tbsp of olive oil into a Dutch oven that has already been heated. Ensure the oven is scorching; a drop of water should pop and sizzle immediately. Take the chicken out of the marinade and use brown sugar to rub it on the outside (SAVE THE MARINADE). Lay the chicken skin side down in the Dutch oven. Cook for 6 to 8 minutes or until the skin is brown and crispy. After that, flip it over and cook for two more minutes.
4. Baking: Take the Dutch oven off the coals and add the marinade. Set up about 9 coals under the Dutch oven's lid and 18 coals on top of the lid. Put the chicken in the oven for about 30 minutes or until it's fully cooked.
5. Serve: It tastes great with rice or pilaf and sauce on top.

84. GARLIC CHICKEN

Prep Time: 10 Minutes | Cook Time: 1 Hour 30 Minutes

Total Time: 1 Hour 40 Minutes | Serving: 6

Ingredients

- ➢ 2 tbsp butter
- ➢ 1 large apple
- ➢ 1 whole chicken - thawed
- ➢ 2 tbsp minced garlic

Glaze:

- ➢ 1 tsp granulated garlic
- ➢ ½ tbsp Dijon mustard
- ➢ 1 tsp black pepper
- ➢ 1/2 tsp kosher salt
- ➢ ¼ cup of molasses

Instructions

1. Warm the oven up to 375 degrees. Spray cooking spray inside the Dutch oven.
2. In the bottom of the pot, put ½ of the garlic. Then add the chicken.
3. Inside the chicken, stuff an apple. Rub the outside with butter and sprinkle the rest of the garlic on top.
4. Put a lid on top and cook for 1½ to 2 hours. After the first hour, check the temperature every 15 minutes. The temperature needs to reach 160 degrees.
5. Make the glaze once the chicken has reached 160 degrees.
6. Mix all the glaze items in a small bowl with a whisk. Then, brush the glaze on the chicken.
7. Leave the chicken in the oven for another 20 to 30 minutes uncovered to let the glaze cook in and the skin get crispy.
8. Take it out and let it sit for 10 minutes before you cut it up and serve it.

85. CAMP OVEN LAMB ROAST WITH VEGETABLES

Prep Time: 30 Minutes | Cook Time: 3 Hour | Total Time: 3 Hour 30 Minutes | Serving: 6

Ingredients

- 1 litre (4 cups) chicken stock
- 500 gram pumpkin, unpeeled, cut into 5cm (2-inch) pieces
- 8 medium_piece (1.6kg) potatoes, halved
- 2 kilogram lamb leg
- 1/3 cup of (80ml) olive oil
- 2 cup of (500ml) water
- 8 clove garlic, unpeeled
- 4 sprigs rosemary

Instructions

1. Warm up the big camp oven.
2. Put the lamb and rosemary in the camp oven. Pour the oil and stock over the lamb and season it. Cover and cook for one and a half hours.
3. Put the pumpkin, potatoes, garlic, and water into the camp oven. Cover and cook for another 1½ hours, or until the lamb is fully cooked.

86. DUTCH OVEN SOUTHWEST CHICKEN

Prep Time: 10 Minutes | Cook Time: 30 Minutes | Total Time: 40 Minutes | Serving: 6

Ingredients

- ¾ cup of sliced green onions
- 2½ cups of chicken cubed
- 1 10¾ ounce can cream of celery soup
- 1 10 ounce can Diced Tomatoes with Green Chilies undrained
- 1 4 ounce can diced green chilies
- 1 tbsp sliced green onions for garnish
- 1 10¾ ounce can cream of mushroom soup
- 2 cups of shredded Cheddar cheese, divided
- 10 flour tortillas (8 inch), cut into small pieces

Instructions

1. Get a fire going or 24 charcoal briquettes ready.
2. Warm up the Dutch oven and add some oil.
3. While the chicken is still hot, brown it and make sure it's fully cooked.
4. Put in the Dutch oven 1 cup of cheese, both soups, tomatoes that have not been drained, green chilies, and ¾ cup of green onions.
5. Break up the tortillas and add them to the Dutch oven.
6. Aim for a simmer after 30 minutes of baking at 350 degrees with 8 coals on the bottom and 10 on the lid.
7. Place the last cup of cheese on top and bake for five minutes, or until the cheese melts.
8. Do not serve until ten to fifteen minutes have passed. Add green onions as a garnish.

87. SPRITE CHICKEN

Prep Time: 20 Minutes | Cook Time: 45 Minutes

Total Time: 1 Hour 5 Minutes | Serving: 10

Ingredients

- ➢ 1 pound petite baby carrots or peeled carrots cut into small pieces
- ➢ ½ pound uncooked bacon, chopped 8 ounces
- ➢ 2 ½ pounds red potatoes cut into 2-inch pieces
- ➢ 1 cup of shredded cheese
- ➢ 1 cup of Sprite or apple juice
- ➢ ½ tbsp seasoning salt like Lawry's
- ➢ 2 onions cut in fourths
- ➢ ½ cup of flour
- ➢ 1 ½ pounds boneless chicken cut into chunks

Instructions

Oven instructions:

1. Warm the oven up to 175°F/350°F.
2. Put the bacon pieces in a large Dutch oven and cook them until crispy. Take the bacon off, but don't throw away the grease.
3. In a gallon bag, mix the flour and seasoning salt together. Put the chicken chunks in the bag and shake it around to coat it. Then, heat the Dutch oven over medium-high heat and brown the chicken in the bacon grease. Take out the chicken.
4. Put the food in the Dutch oven that is now empty in this order: onions first, then potatoes, carrots, chicken, and bacon. Then pour Sprite over everything.
5. Put the lid on the Dutch oven and bake for 45 to 55 minutes, or until the carrots and potatoes are soft. Add cheese shreds on top and serve.

Camping Dutch Oven Instructions:

9. Follow the steps above to get the ingredients ready. Then, put the Dutch oven on 11 hot coals in the shape of a checker board. Put 17 hot coals on top of the oven's lid. That's 320 degrees 45 minutes to cook. Take off the lid. Put cheese on top. Replace the lid. Bring it back to a boil. Do it.

88. CHICKEN BLACK BEAN CHILI

Prep Time: 5 Minutes | Cook Time: 20 Minutes | Total Time: 30 Minutes | Serving: 6

Ingredients

- 1 package ranch dressing mix
- 1 can corn
- 1 package taco seasoning mix
- 1 can black beans
- 1 can white beans
- 1 cup of salsa
- 2 stalks celery
- 2 cans of chunk chicken (25 ounce)
- 1 block cream cheese

Instructions

1. Get the celery clean and cut it up. First, open the black beans and chicken and drain them. Then, add them to the pot.
2. Open the can of extra beans and corn and pour the whole thing into the pot.
3. Put the salsa in. Add the contents of the packets and mix them in. Put in pieces of cream cheese. About 20 minutes of steaming on medium heat should break up the cream cheese. We cooked outside by the fire.

89. LATIN CAMPFIRE CHICKEN

Prep Time: 15 Minutes | Cook Time: 1 Hour 5 Minutes

Total Time: 1 Hour 20 Minutes | Serving: 4

Ingredients

- 1/2 tsp allspice
- 1/2 tsp salt
- 1/4 tsp pepper
- 2 tsp ground cumin
- 2 pounds boneless skinless chicken breasts cubed
- 4 garlic cloves minced
- 1/2 cup of chicken broth
- 1 large sweet potato peeled
- 1 cup of prepared hot salsa
- 2 (15 ounce) cans black beans
- 1 red bell pepper chopped
- 1 bunch fresh cilantro chopped

Instructions

1. You can measure and mix the ingredients marked with an asterisk at home.
2. Set up the campfire so that you can cook over low heat. You can also use charcoal briquettes or a camp stove that runs on propane.
3. In a 12-inch camp Dutch oven, mix the chicken, salsa, broth, cumin, allspice, salt, pepper, garlic, sweet potato, bell pepper, and beans.
4. Cover and cook on medium-low heat for 45 to 60 minutes or until the potatoes are soft and the chicken is cooked.
5. Now, take off the lid and cook without it for about 20 to 30 minutes, or until all the liquid is absorbed and the sauce gets thick. Add cilantro on top, and serve.

90. LAMB PEKA

Prep Time: 30 Minutes | Cook Time: 2 Hour 10 Minutes

Total Time: 2 Hour 40 Minutes | Serving: 6

Ingredients

- 1 1/2 pounds large carrots, trimmed and cut into 3-inch pieces
- 1 tsp ground black pepper, divided
- 1 tbsp kosher salt, divided
- 2 large yellow onions, cut into 1 1/2-inch wedges
- Flaky sea salt, for serving
- 2 pounds small Yukon Gold potatoes, halved if larger than 2 1/2 inches in diameter
- 1 head garlic, cloves peeled
- 4 rosemary sprigs
- 1 cup of dry white wine
- 6 tbsp extra-virgin olive oil, divided, plus more for serving
- 6 bone-in lamb neck chops or shoulder chops (about 8 ounces each)

Instructions

To prepare this recipe using your oven:

1. Warm the oven up to 350°F. Put a single layer of potatoes on the bottom of a 12-inch, 8-quart Dutch oven. Put onions, garlic, and carrots on top of the potatoes. Put one tsp of salt and half a tsp of pepper. Take rosemary leaves off of sprigs and sprinkle them on vegetables. Put 3 tbsp of olive oil on top.
2. Add the last two tsp of salt and the last half tsp of pepper to the lamb. Put the lamb chops on the vegetables and drizzle with the last 3 tbsp of oil. Cover and bake in an oven for about an hour or until it browns.
3. Please remove the lid and carefully turn the lamb and vegetables over so they don't burn. Put the lid back on, add the wine, and put the pan back in the oven. Keep cooking for another 45 minutes to an hour or until a fork can go through the vegetables easily and the lamb is soft enough to pull off the bone. Take off the lid and cook for 10 to 15 minutes, until the lamb is browned. Serve straight from the pot, with extra olive oil and flaky sea salt on top.

To prepare this recipe using a charcoal grill:

1. Light two charcoal chimney starters that are half full of briquettes. Put 1 chimney starter's worth of briquettes on the bottom of a charcoal grill when the briquettes are covered in gray ash. The bottom grate should go on top of the charcoal.
2. Set the potatoes in a single layer on the bottom of a 12-inch, 8-quart cast-iron Dutch oven with a flanged lid while the charcoal heats up. Put onions, garlic, and carrots on

top of the potatoes. For each vegetable, add one tsp of salt and half a tsp of pepper. Take rosemary leaves off of sprigs and sprinkle them on vegetables. Put 3 tbsp of olive oil on top. Add the last two tsp of salt and the last half tsp of pepper to the lamb.

3. Place the lamb on top of the vegetables and drizzle with the last 3 tbsp of oil. Cover the Dutch oven on top of the bottom grill grate. Spread a thin layer of the charcoal that is left over the Dutch oven's lid. For about an hour, cook until the lamb starts to turn brown. Light one more charcoal chimney starter that is half full of briquettes to save for later use.

4. Take care to scrape the charcoal off of the lid. Take off the lid and flip the vegetables and lamb to keep them from burning. Put the lid back on, add the wine, and then add another thin layer of charcoal on top of the lid. Keep cooking for another 30 to 45 minutes until a fork into a vegetable turns soft and the lamb is just soft enough to pull away from the bone. Take it off the grill and serve it right from the pot, with extra olive oil and flaky sea salt on top.

To prepare this recipe over an open fire:

1. A hardwood campfire should be built in a fire pit about an hour before cooking. The fire should be left to burn down to red-hot coals, which should then turn into smaller, ash-covered glowing embers. Now you're ready to start cooking.

2. Put potatoes on the bottom of a 12-inch, 8-quart cast-iron Dutch oven with a lid that has a lip around the edge. Put onions, garlic, and carrots on top of the potatoes. Mix in one tsp of salt and half a tsp of pepper. Take rosemary leaves off of sprigs and sprinkle them on vegetables. Put 3 tbsp of olive oil on top. Add the last two tsp of salt and the last half tsp of pepper to the lamb.

3. Place the lamb on top of the vegetables and drizzle with the last 3 tbsp of oil. Cover the pot. When the embers are ready, move some of them to the side of the fire pit so that there is a thin, even layer. That's where you should put the pot. By spreading out some of the remaining embers on top of the lid, you can make the Dutch oven feel like an oven. Take an hour to cook. In the meantime, pile up the extra embers around the edge of the fire pit and add a little more wood to start a small fire in case you need more embers later.

4. After an hour, carefully take the lid off and remove the embers from the lid. Add the wine and turn the meat over to brown the other side. Note if it's cooking evenly, and if it isn't, turn the pot or add more embers. Put the lid back on and add embers to the top. It will take 30 to 45 minutes of cooking until the meat and vegetables are very soft when poked with a fork.

5. Brush the embers off the lid, then take it off. Take the pot off the fire pit while wearing heavy-duty oven mitts or grilling gloves that can handle the heat. Serve straight from the pot, with extra olive oil and flaky sea salt on top.

91. PEACH COBBLER

Prep Time: 10 Minutes | Cook Time: 30 Minutes

Total Time: 40 Minutes | Serving: 6

Ingredients

Filling:

➤ 6-8 ripe peaches
➤ 2 tbsp sugar

Topping:

➤ ½ tsp salt
➤ ½ cup of butter, melted
➤ ½ cup of sugar, 60g
➤ 1 tsp baking powder
➤ 1 cup of flour, 120g
➤ whipped cream, optional

Instructions

1. Light your charcoal briquettes or start a campfire so you have embers to work with. Put a round of parchment paper inside the Dutch oven.
2. Put the butter in a metal or enamel bowl and set it next to the campfire to melt.
3. Cut the peaches into small pieces that you can easily eat. Add them to the Dutch oven that has been lined with foil and sprinkle with 2 tbsp of sugar.
4. In a bowl, baking powder, mix the flour, salt, and the rest of the sugar.
5. Mix the butter with the dry ingredients after it melts. Carefully mix with a fork until the mixture is soft and crumbly.
6. Cover the peaches in the Dutch oven with the crumbly topping. Put the lid on top.
7. Place the Dutch oven on top of the fire ring. To get the oven to about 350F, put 7 coals in a circle under it and 14 coals on top of the lid. Put it in the oven for 20 to 30 minutes, or until the topping is golden and the filling is bubbling. If they start to cool down, you might need to add more coals.
8. Take it out of the fire and serve it with whipped cream.

92. PINEAPPLE UPSIDE DOWN CAKE

Prep Time: 15 Minutes | Cook Time: 30 Minutes

Total Time: 45 Minutes | Serving: 8-10

Ingredients

- 2 tbsp light brown sugar
- ½ cup of thick plain Greek yogurt
- ¼ cup of pineapple juice
- ¾ cup of granulated sugar
- 1 ½ cup of all-purpose flour
- 7 pineapple rings, canned or fresh
- 21 maraschino cherries
- 1 ½ tsp ground cinnamon
- ½ cup of extra virgin olive oil
- 1 tsp vanilla extract
- ½ tsp baking powder
- ⅛ tsp salt
- 3 large eggs

Instructions

1. Put 20 charcoal briquettes in a fire ring or some other container that can't catch fire.
2. Light the briquettes and let them heat up for twenty to thirty minutes.
3. To make the sauce smooth, mix the olive oil and sugar in a large bowl with a whisk.
4. Add the yogurt, pineapple juice, eggs, and vanilla extract and mix them in well.
5. To make the dough smooth and well mixed, add the flour, salt, baking powder, and eggs and mix them all together. Put aluminum foil around the sides and bottom of your 10-inch cast iron Dutch oven. You can skip this step, but it makes cleanup a lot easier.
6. Line the bottom of your Dutch oven with seven pineapple rings, spaced out evenly.
7. Put a maraschino cherry in the middle of each pineapple ring and any empty spots on the Dutch oven's bottom.
8. On top of the pineapple and cherries, spread out the brown sugar and cinnamon.
9. Put 12 of the hot charcoal briquettes in a fire ring or fire safe pan. Place the Dutch oven on top of the hot coals.
10. Over the pineapple slices, spread out the cake batter, and then put the lid on top of the Dutch oven.
11. Spread out the last eight hot charcoal briquettes on top of the Dutch oven's lid. Bake for another 30 minutes, or until the cake is done.
12. Take the Dutch oven off the heat and take off the lid. During that time, let the cake cool down. Place a plate with the right side down on top of the Dutch oven.
13. Because the pot is still hot, carefully flip the Dutch oven over so that it rests on top of the plate. Make sure to use oven mitts for this.
14. Slowly take the Dutch oven off the plate, making sure the cake stays on the plate as you do so. Take care to remove the foil from the cake. Warm up or let it sit out before serving.

93. BLUEBERRY COBBLER

Prep Time: 10 Minutes | Cook Time: 45 Minutes

Total Time: 55 Minutes | Serving: 4

Ingredients

Filling:

- ➤ 1 tbsp flour
- ➤ 3 cups of fresh Oregon blueberries
- ➤ 1 tsp ground cinnamon
- ➤ Juice & zest from ½ lemon, about 1 tbsp juice
- ➤ 2 tbsp sugar

Topping:

- ➤ ¼ cup of sugar, (60g)
- ➤ ¼ cup of butter, cold
- ➤ ½ tsp salt
- ➤ ⅓ cup of milk
- ➤ 1 cup of flour, (140g)
- ➤ 1 tsp baking powder
- ➤ Optional: whipped cream

Instructions

1. To make the filling, put the blueberries, sugar, flour, cinnamon, and the juice and zest of half a lemon in a bowl and toss to coat.
2. Put the blueberry mix into a 4-quart Dutch oven that has been lined.
3. Add the flour, salt, baking powder, and sugar in a bowl and mix them together to make the mix. Fry the butter and flour together until they are about the size of peas. You can use a fork or your hands to do this. Mix everything together after you add the milk.
4. Spread the batter for the topping over the blueberries.
5. Place the Dutch oven on a bed of seven coals and add fourteen more to the lid of the oven.
6. Once every 15 minutes, turn the oven and lid ¼ turn and add more coals if they run out. Cook for another 40 to 45 minutes, or until the topping is golden brown.
7. Take the dish off the heat and leave it out to cool a bit before adding whipped cream.

94. CHOCOLATE CAKE

Prep Time: 5 Minutes | Cook Time: 24 Minutes | Additional Time: 6 Minute

Total Time: 35 Minutes | Serving: 12

Ingredients

- Devil's Food Cake Mix
- Can of Lemon-Lime Soda
- Chocolate Chips
- Mini Marshmallows

Instructions

1. Get coals hot for the Dutch oven.
2. Spray cooking spray on the foil that you put inside the Dutch oven.
3. Put the soda to the cake mix and mix them together.
4. Put the mini marshmallows and chocolate chips to the batter and mix them in.
5. About half of a bag of chips and a third of a bag of marshmallows were all we used.
6. The batter should be spread out in the Dutch oven.
7. If you have a high heat, put the lid on the Dutch oven and cover it with coals. Bake for 24 to 30 minutes. You can tell when it's done by the smell. At 29 minutes, we took it out.
8. How long it takes will depend on how big your Dutch oven is and how hot the coals are.

95. TURTLE LAVA CAKE

Prep Time: 5 Minutes | Cook Time: 40 Minutes | Additional Time: 15

Total Time: 1 Hour | Serving: 12

Ingredients

- One package of chocolate chips
- One cup of whole pecans
- One Devil's food cake mix
- One jar of caramel sauce
- One can of lemon-lime soda

Instructions

1. Using the charcoal chimney, get about 18 pieces of charcoal ready.
2. Put a Dutch oven liner inside the oven. Put the caramel sauce in the Dutch oven's bottom. Put the cake mix on top of the caramel. Pour the soda over the cake mix slowly.
3. Put the chocolate chips from the bag on top of the cake mix.
4. Put the pecans on top of the chocolate chips. Cover your touch oven with the lid.
5. Set up six pieces of charcoal in a circle under your Dutch oven.
6. Please put the last of the charcoal on the Dutch oven's lid.
7. It was baked for 40 to 55 minutes, based on how your nose tells you. Watch out to bake only a little bit! Enjoy!

96. BLACKBERRY PEACH CRISP

Prep Time: 30 Minutes | Cook Time: 40 Minutes

Total Time: 1 Hour 10 Minutes | Serving: 4

Ingredients

Topping:

- 1/4 cup of packed brown sugar
- 1/4 tsp nutmeg
- 2/3 cup of all-purpose flour
- 1/3 cup of quick-cooking oats
- 1 stick of unsalted butter
- 1/4 cup of raw sesame seeds
- 1/4 tsp salt

Fruit Filling:

- 3 Tbsp brown sugar
- 1/2 pint blackberries
- 4 ripe peaches
- juice of 1/2 lemon
- zest of 1 lemon

Instructions

1. Get your charcoal briquettes hot. It depends on how big your Dutch oven is. Assuming you want to bake at 400°F, you will need 17 briquettes on top of your 10-inch Dutch oven and 8 on the bottom. Additionally, I always heat a few extra.
2. Paper towels make cleaning a cast iron Dutch oven a breeze. Take the peaches and cut them up. Layer the blackberries and peaches and put them in the Dutch oven.
3. Include the zest of one lemon, the juice of half a lemon, and three tbsp of brown sugar. Use the mix to cover the fruit well.
4. Put the topping mix you made at home in a large bowl. After breaking up a stick of butter into small pieces, mix it with the topping mix.
5. Using your hands or two forks to break up the butter into the flour mixture is okay.
6. The mixture should be spread out evenly over the fruit. Attach the lid to the Dutch oven.
7. As soon as the briquettes are hot, put some under the Dutch oven and some on top of the lid to make the inside 400°F. After 40 minutes, turn the Dutch oven 180° and cook for another 40 minutes.
8. After the cooking is done, carefully take out the briquettes and open the lid to see a lovely Dutch oven crisp. Assemble and enjoy!

97. CHOCOLATE CHERRY LAVA CAKE

Prep Time: 20 Minutes | Cook Time: 50 Minutes | Additional Time: 10

Total Time: 1 Hour 20 Minutes | Serving:

Ingredients

- ➤ chocolate cake mix, 1 box
- ➤ chocolate chips, 1 bag
- ➤ cherry pie filling, 1 can
- ➤ lemon-lime soda, 1 12 ounce can

Instructions

1. Get 24 or more pieces of charcoal ready.
2. Put a liner in the Dutch oven or spray it with cooking oil.
3. Put the pie filling in the bottom of the Dutch oven after opening the can.
4. On top of the cherry filling, put the chocolate cake mix.
5. Pour the soda over the cake mix slowly after opening the bottle. You should be able to go slowly and still get foam. Add the chocolate chips to the soda.
6. Cover the Dutch oven with the lid. Put 16 pieces of charcoal on top of the oven's lid.
7. Make a circle with eight charcoal briquettes. This will be the base of the fire for baking the cake.
8. Cover the circle with the Dutch oven and bake the cake for about an hour. How much you use will depend on the size of your Dutch oven and how hot the coals are.
9. Take the Dutch oven off the coals and eat.

98. CAKE & BERRY CAMPFIRE COBBLER

Prep Time: 10 Minutes | Cook Time: 30 Minutes

Total Time: 40 Minutes | Serving: 12

Ingredients

- 2 cans (21 ounces each) raspberry pie filling
- 1-1/4 cups of water
- 1/2 cup of canola oil
- 1 package yellow cake mix
- Vanilla ice cream, optional

Instructions

1. Set the grill or campfire to low heat and add 16 to 20 charcoal briquettes or big wood chips.
2. Heavy-duty aluminum foil should be used to line an oven-safe Dutch oven. Then, add the pie filling. Put the cake mix, water, and oil in a large bowl and mix them together. Cover the pie filling with it.
3. Put a lid on the Dutch oven. Once there is white ash on top of the briquettes or wood chips, put the Dutch oven right on top of 8-13 of them. Put the last few briquettes on the pan cover using tongs with long handles.
4. It takes 30 to 40 minutes of cooking until the topping is golden and a toothpick stuck in the filling comes out clean. Carefully lift the cover with the tongs to see if it's done. Serve with ice cream if you want.

99. BROWNIES

Prep Time: 5 Minutes | Cook Time: 45 Minutes | Additional Time: 15

Total Time: 1 Hour 5 Minutes | Serving: 12

Ingredients

- 12 ounce bag of chocolate chips
- 1 can of dark soda pop
- 1 18.3 ounce box of brownie mix

Instructions

1. Get the coal ready for the Dutch oven.
2. Cover the Dutch oven with a sheet.
3. Add the soda to the brownie mix and stir.
4. Just put the batter in the oven.
5. Put the chocolate chips in the middle of the batter from the bag.
6. Could you put it in the oven for 30 to 60 minutes?

100. TEXAS PEACH COBBLER

Prep Time: 30 Minutes | Cook Time: 45 Minutes

Total Time: 1 Hour 15 Minutes | Serving: 10

Ingredients

- 1 egg beaten
- 5 tbsp very cold water
- 3 cups of flour
- 1 tsp salt
- 1 tbsp white distilled vinegar
- 1 1/2 cups of shortening

Filling:

- 1/2 cup of half and half
- 2 29 ounce cans Sliced Peaches in Heavy Syrup drained
- 1 cup of brown sugar
- 1 tsp cinnamon
- 1 cup of sugar
- 1 cup of butter melted

Instructions

To Prepare the crust:

1. Put the flour in a large bowl. Using a pastry cutter, cut in the shortening until the mixture looks like big crumbs.
2. Stir in the egg, water, vinegar, and salt until everything is mixed.
3. Form into a ball and put it in a large gallon-sized ziplock bag.
4. It should be rolled out inside the bag until it reaches the sides. Then, put it flat in the freezer. Do it again for the second crust.

For the Filling:

1. Add the peaches that have been drained to the sugar and cinnamon.
2. Melt the butter and add the half-and-half. Mix well.
3. Wait until the crust is ready.

To Assemble:

1. Take the crusts out of the freezer and give them 15 minutes to thaw. 2. Make the first crust at least as big as the Dutch oven's bottom.
2. Spray cooking oil on a 12- or 14-inch dutch oven and put the crust in the bottom. Cut it to fit.
3. Put your filling in there. Use a pizza cutter to cut the second crust into 1-inch strips after rolling it out. Criss-cross the pie crust strips on the ground.
4. You can add the great state of Texas to the top of the cobbler if you want to. Use a Texas State cookie cutter to cut a design from the extra pie crust.
5. In a small bowl, beat one egg. Then, use a pastry brush to paint the whole top of the cobbler.
6. Put about 1/4 cup of white sugar and cinnamon.
7. If baking in the oven, leave the lid off and bake at 350 degrees for about 45 minutes.

If cooking outside:

1. Put the lid on top of the Dutch oven.
2. If you have never used a Dutch oven outside, charcoal briquettes might give you more consistent results than coals from a campfire. Use a chimney starter to light half of a 5-pound bag of charcoal. Dump the briquettes on dry ground or a steel table as soon as the edges and corners start to turn gray.
3. With a pair of tongs, spread out 14 briquettes in an area about the size of the bottom of the Dutch oven. Set the Dutch oven on top of the coals. Put a ring of coals around the lid so that the coals touch each other. There should be about 19 or 20 coals in the ring. Put six to seven more coals in a circle around the lid's lift handle in the middle.
4. Set the timer now! Every 10 minutes, carefully lift the Dutch oven off the coals and turn it counterclockwise by 1/4 turn. Put it back on the coals. Do not lift the lid; instead, turn it 1/4 turn clockwise. This way of turning your Dutch oven gets rid of "hot spots" and makes the food cook more evenly.
5. For forty minutes, keep turning the oven and lid in opposite directions every ten minutes. After that, carefully lift the lid and look to see if the crust is starting to turn brown. Check on it every five minutes until it turns golden brown.
6. When it's done, take it off the coals and carefully take off the lid!! Allow to cool for five to ten minutes before serving.

fc241ca3-1f01-4683-8fd6-5fd7da0dbb35R01